FULL RECOVERY

FULL RECOVERY

The Recovering Person's Guide to Unleashing Your Inner Power

BRIAN McALISTER

MacSimum Publishing Company

Author's note: The information given in this book is designed to help you make informed decisions about your recovery. It is not intended as a substitute for any treatment program. Treatment is available at Full Recovery Wellness Center, Fairfield, NJ. This book presents principles widely accepted by all theologies and civilizations, but rarely understood or utilized.

The events described in this book are real. In the spirit of anonymity, all names—excluding the author's—and locations have been changed to protect the privacy of the people discussed.

Published by MacSimum Publishing Company
Hampton, New Jersey

Distributed by Greenleaf Book Group

For ordering information or special discounts for bulk purchases, please contact Greenleaf Book Group at PO Box 91869, Austin, TX 78709, 512.891.6100.

Design and composition by Greenleaf Book Group and Bumpy Design
Cover design by MacSimum Publishing LLC and Rory McAlister

Publisher's Cataloging-In-Publication Data
McAlister, Brian.
Full recovery: the recovering person's guide to unleashing your inner power/Brian McAlister. —Third edition.
pages ; cm
ISBN: 978-0-9823948-2-3
1. Recovering addicts—Conduct of life. 2. Addicts—Rehabilitation. 3. Conduct of life. 4. Self-actualization (Psychology) 5. Success—Psychological aspects. I. Title.

HV4998 .M33 2015
362.291/86

Originally published as 978-0-9823948-0-9

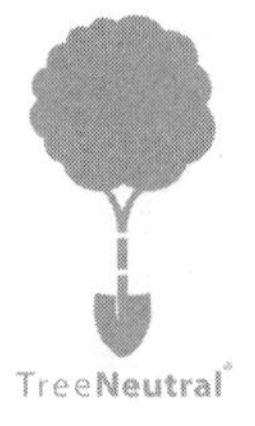

Part of the Tree Neutral® program, which offsets the number of trees consumed in the production and printing of this book by taking proactive steps, such as planting trees in direct proportion to the number of trees used: www.treeneutral.com.

Printed in the United States of America on acid-free paper.

15 16 17 18 19 20 21   10 9 8 7 6 5 4 3 2 1

Third Edition

Acknowledgments

To my son, Rory, and my beautiful wife, Paula, your continuous love and support allow me to experience my full potential. Mom, Dad, Eddie, and Elaine, your encouragement means more than you know. Thanks to Uncle Matt, Brian Ford, Bill Agne, Lynda and Ben Kinsley, and Laurie Kessler for your constructive feedback; Sheila, Tommy, Carl, Aunt Margaret, Uncle Charles, and everyone else who helps me remember where I came from. Bobby U., I love your enthusiasm. My sister Sharon, and all the others who didn't make it: you are missed . . . and lastly my grandmother, Mary O'Brien, the endless prayers from your lips to God's ears helped keep me alive long enough to get sober.

I love you all.

Contents

Introduction 1

Part I—Exploration

Open Your Mind 15

What you need to know about how life really works. Every act rewards itself. Setbacks are the prelude to success. The relationship between adversity and opportunity. Turn hope into faith.

Know Yourself 31

Separate your talents and assets from your fantasies and defects. Understand the power of choice and the consequences of not choosing. Learn how to ask better questions in order to receive better answers.

Fear 43

Living in fear is seductive and habit-forming. Fear wears many masks and hides behind many emotions. Learn ways of overcoming fear, negativity, and rejection.

Perceptions 65

The ego can distort reality and your beliefs can influence your perceptions. Question long-standing beliefs. Learn common roadblocks to full recovery, springboards to abundance, and reprogram your mind for success.

The Gift of Discomfort 91

Understand the pain/pleasure principle and how you can use it to instantly improve your life. Create new empowering habits. You become what you think about.

Part II—Motivation

Develop Abundance Awareness 115
Define your own concept of abundance: love, health, sobriety, family, money, peace of mind. Prayer and meditation are essential to raising your consciousness. More service to others equals more personal success in your life.

Gratitude—Wants—Needs 133
Being grateful shifts your reality. Learn easy ways to break unproductive thinking patterns. Discover the difference between wants and needs. Determine what you want and why you really want it.

Live Inspired 155
Turn your God-given desires into reality. Tap into your creativity and find solutions to your own and our shared societal problems. Move beyond self-imposed limitations.

Live Your Truth 177
Learn how to avoid the dangers of an ego-driven life and realize the power in your words. Through knowledge, education, and effective communication skills, you can leverage this power.

Part III—Dedication

GPS: Goals Produce Success 191
Turn your character defects into assets. Learn how to turn goals into reality. Huge goals create huge inspiration.

Your Project 211
Choose one life-affirming project. Explore the character traits needed for long-term success in recovery. Key concepts: enthusiasm, commitment, perseverance, and accomplishment.

Deliberate Action 229

Move your dreams of an abundant, full recovery onto the broad highway of success through action. Be a problem solver rather than being a manipulator. Overcome obstacles, schedule appointments, market your ideas, close the deal, and respect your customer/audience.

A Moment of Clarity 247

Explains how the spiritual and material worlds are interconnected. Call it grace, a hunch, a gut feeling, or premonitions—we all have contact with the universal consciousness. Will you answer "yes" to life?

Introduction

Today, you are beginning a life-changing experience. You may be in a recovery program or simply wish to make positive changes, but are you struggling to take the next step and experience life in all its richness? This book will show you how to take that step and realize your dreams.

Your dreams of abundance will become reality if you simply make a commitment to listen and take action. My definition of abundance goes far beyond money and material wealth. It includes love, truth, health, spiritual prosperity, and peace of mind. You will be given the tools to awaken within you the ability to create a compelling future and achieve your destiny.

Addiction of any kind is the opposite of freedom and in no way resembles abundant living. It is a habit rooted in self-deception and fear. Addiction occupies your focus and hijacks your consciousness. It deludes you into believing you can deceive yourself and others. Duplicity promotes anxiety and fear that mutates into depression and guilt. Addiction interferes with your creative impulses. It prohibits you from being able to organize your good ideas in any meaningful way. You are unable to stay productive or exercise any rational choice regarding your actions or enterprise because your focus is constantly being drawn away from your dreams and toward your addiction.

The paradox of addiction is that in your attempt to empower yourself through artificial means, you actually give up your free will to those outside forces you turned to for empowerment. The very thing you use to grant yourself control over your unpleasant internal state becomes the cause of your internal distress.

The reality is that although fear and addiction can destroy your connection with your creativity, they cannot destroy your potential to do great things. Your potential is a freely given birthright and part of your destiny. Your ability to create and achieve is a choice. As with creativity, recovery is also a choice. It is right thinking. It is soundness of thought and action. Recovery allows you to realign the misguided perception of the material world, which your ego has created, with the true nature of the universe in all its splendor.

The suggestions I offer in this book are designed to take you beyond abstinence and give you the personal insight needed to realign those misguided perceptions that have been holding you back.

You will learn the skills needed to trade addiction for inspiration. By answering the thought-provoking questions I pose in each chapter, you will gain the awareness and introspection needed to reach your full potential. By picking up this book, you have made a choice to embark on a life of unlimited possibilities.

I would venture a guess that this is not the first time you have heard about reaching your full potential, but what does that statement actually mean? The word *potential* is derived from the root word *potent*, which means powerful, or wielding force, authority, or influence. Potential is defined as that which is possible and able to be developed into actuality. Think about what the definition of potential means for you. It says you are empowered; you have authority over your decisions and your life; you are capable of developing into the person you actually want to be; you are a force to be reckoned with. Now that you've chosen recovery, the only limits to your potential are the restrictions you put on yourself and your own creativity. The miracle of recovery is that you can choose—right now . . . today—to reach your full potential.

You might be thinking, "Well, that sounds good, but I'm already too old" or "I don't have the education" or "I've had bad breaks" or any number of fearful excuses that keep you stagnant and unfulfilled. Remember this: You are not old until your regrets replace your dreams.

Old is a very subjective term. When I was in my early thirties, I was physically and mentally old. Twenty years of alcohol and drug abuse had extinguished my dreams. Regrets and depression had replaced the confidence of youth. I felt I had squandered my opportunities. I lacked a formal education, had no marketable skills, and due to my alcoholism and other addictions was unable to hold down a job. Suicidal thoughts were repressed by intoxication to the point of blacking out. A sense of overwhelming, impending doom haunted me. How did I get to that place? What had happened to me? Let me explain.

Remember this: You are not old until your regrets replace your dreams.

As a child, I grew up in a blue-collar town with blue-collar values. People worked hard and played hard. I was taught never to be afraid or, worse, to show fear. If you were afraid to fight or you showed fear, you were going to have a very rough time. I learned to play many roles and wear many disguises. At an early age, I started admiring and imitating people who seemed to have no fear. Little did I know at the time that ignorance, alcohol, and drug abuse often mask fear.

My formative years were in the late 1960s and early 1970s. Alcohol and drug use were very much a part of the counterculture. Once I tried them . . . so was I.

Fear left me. I would live by my own rules. I would be a rebel, defiant. I would play God. As a child, I was taught that children are to be seen and not heard. I decided I would be heard.

All through my twenties, I lived an outlaw biker lifestyle. My world revolved around getting high and riding my Harley. I was intoxicated 24/7. I was involved in many violent altercations. I used my living room as my garage. That's right; I would drive my Harley right through the front door and park it on the living room carpet. I would tell my wife it was just to make sure it didn't get stolen. How's that for self-justification!

By medicating myself with drugs and alcohol, my consciousness of right and wrong became blurred. The choices I made created the life I was living. The seeds I had sown bore rotten fruit. The results were self-evident. I was an alcoholic, drug-addicted biker. My family life and marriage were deplorable, and my finances even worse. I had been in several severe car and motorcycle accidents, some with prolonged hospital stays. I was basically unemployable and praying for the end.

Make that *hoping* for the end because, at the time, I did not acknowledge the existence of God or any other higher power. God and I had a falling out years earlier when the concept of the forgiving Christ and the "turn the other cheek" lectures I had endured were pitted against the reality of my being permanently expelled from a Catholic high school for what I considered a minor offense. The situation smelled of hypocrisy and I would not accept it. Instead, I nurtured a resentment that almost killed me and simply made everyone else I came into contact with miserable.

My wife and my son were exposed to a low-rent lifestyle they neither wanted nor deserved. My life was on a downward spiral and I saw no way out.

Rather than taking responsibility for my actions, I managed to convince myself that my wife was really the problem. If I could just get away from her nagging, I wouldn't have to drink and drug so much. So I made arrangements to leave my wife and small son on the West Coast and head back east. Luckily, providence intervened. I had a horrible accident, the effects of which are still being realized today. Out of that tragedy has grown a way of life so infinitely rewarding that I could not have imagined it possible while in the depths of my addiction. It has resulted in a complete transformation of ideas and concepts that are the basis for this book. And I can say with complete confidence that what you'll read here will lead you to a higher awareness and an exceptional life in recovery. You are standing at the threshold of unlimited possibility. It's time to take action and step through the doorway.

History gives us many other examples of outstanding results achieved by people considered old or uneducated by society's standards. Colonel Sanders, the founder of Kentucky Fried

Chicken, didn't start selling his famous chicken recipe with eleven herbs and spices until after he retired from the post office. His dissatisfaction with his income and his way of life drove him to create one of the largest and most successful restaurant chains in the world.

Another great example is Albert Einstein. As hard as it might be for you to believe, Einstein was unable to find employment as a teacher upon graduating from college. His professors refused to give him a letter of recommendation, which at that time was a requirement for being hired as a teacher. They considered him lazy, and one professor had actually failed him in physics. Einstein settled for a job in the government patent office reviewing applications. It was during this low point in his life that he developed the theories that revolutionized the science of physics and transformed our understanding of the universe.

These men are but two people who decided to reach their potential. Maybe life has been preparing you for just this moment to achieve abundance.

Ted's Journey to Full Recovery

I know a man whom I'll call Ted in order to protect his anonymity. Ted entered his mid-thirties as a low-bottom alcoholic and drug addict. The day finally came when Ted could no longer stomach this depressing lifestyle, and he decided to do whatever it took to get sober.

After seeking treatment and staying sober, he set his sights on achieving full recovery. Ted decided to realize his full potential. He had always been interested in the medical field and decided to be a volunteer emergency medical worker. He studied and became an EMT. Ted felt proud of his accomplishment and found his job of helping people rewarding, but his newfound confidence gave him an appetite to reach higher. Ted was ready for a bigger challenge, so he went back to school and studied to become a nurse. As a nurse Ted excelled and always surpassed the expectations of his patients and doctors, but before too long, he once again came to the realization that he still was not reaching his full potential.

Ted learned through the miracle of sobriety that with God, all things are possible, but he did not stop with that realization. He took action. Even though he had little money and was then in his mid-forties, he made a decision to become a doctor. The noun *decision* comes from the verb *to decide,* whose Latin root, *decidere,* means to cut away. Ted decided at that moment to cut away from his limiting beliefs.

Many naysayers were only too happy to give their opinions. They told him he was too old to start training to be a doctor; he would never get into medical school with his background; he would be in his fifties by the time he graduated; he couldn't afford it. But Ted had made a life-altering decision—a decision to reach his full potential.

He applied to every medical school in the USA. He then searched the whole world over looking for a school willing to give him a chance. Finally, he received a letter that he had been accepted into a school in Latin America.

Ted left the United States and moved to a Third World country. It was not an easy situation. He had very little money and lived in substandard housing. Yet, through it all, he let nothing distract him, kept true to his goal to be a doctor, and persevered.

I recently ran into Ted. Having graduated from medical

school, he was currently employed by an international nonprofit providing free medical care to the poor.

Ted is in his fifties now, just as the naysayers had predicted; the difference is that Ted reached that age as a doctor. He would have been in his fifties either way, but Ted arrived fulfilled and happy, having achieved his goal, as opposed to depressed and full of regret for not having tried. Ted is a true inspiration. He is an example of what making a decision and keeping a commitment to a full recovery can mean for you.

Ted recognized the enormous opportunities and unlimited potential this experience we call life has to offer. Think about it for a moment. To be living in the Western Hemisphere in the twenty-first century is truly a blessing. Our standard of living is the highest in recorded history. The luxuries we take for granted today would have been considered miracles, or impossible, only a few short decades ago. We have access to the very best health care, education, technology, and material comforts, yet many of us still live an unfulfilled, fearful existence. Lack of direction, coupled with incessant worrying, dilutes our self-esteem. Depression and addiction have become the plagues of our modern time. Untreated addiction is responsible for untold misery and loss.

I know what I'm talking about. When I was a young man, addictions, fear, lack, and ignorance were my constant companions. My experience in this world of addiction is in such sharp contrast to the life of abundance I currently enjoy that it almost feels as though it were another lifetime ago . . . and in a lot of ways, it was. I believe that I have been catapulted into a new enlightened existence. I have been granted the best deal ever: two lives for the price of one. The best part is that this deal is available to anyone willing to take the same simple and enlightening journey.

What unfolds in the three parts of this book is what I like to call "the journey to full recovery." In Part I—Exploration, you'll start by digging deep to discover the habits and beliefs that led to your poor decision making in the past. You will learn effective ways of overcoming fear, reprogramming your mind for success, and avoiding relapse.

In Part II—Motivation, I provide effective exercises that help you discover what truly motivates you. You decide if your present course is right or wrong. Do you want to chart a new course? You learn how to develop a better internal dialogue and jump-start your own idea of abundant recovery. You'll pinpoint obstacles you are currently facing, and learn how they can be overcome. You'll learn effective ways to communicate your intentions and attract people capable of helping you.

In the final section, Part III—Dedication, you will define and develop a game plan for accomplishing one substantial life-improving personal project. You will learn the time-tested ethical standards and character traits needed for *long-term* success. You will be given the tools to overcome hurdles and real-life challenges. You will discover ways of communicating with secretaries and support staff that will open previously locked doors. I'll teach you the skills needed to schedule appointments, market your ideas, ask for a raise, or start a business. You will learn how the same skill set needed to maintain sobriety could be used to advance your career and strengthen personal relationships.

I want to stress that reading this book is a great beginning, but reaching your full potential will require your participation. I will be asking you many questions, and you will have to write down the answers to all of them in order to get the desired results. I speak to you in a language that is easily understood, and the exercises will provide measurable results. I promise that I have done my best not to waste any of your time with unimportant details.

You will need a notebook or electronic device, of course, to save your answers and to do the work explained in the exercises. So, right now, go and get yourself a notebook or open a file and write the words *Full Recovery Action Plan*. Each and every time you read through a chapter, make sure to have your Full Recovery Action Plan handy. It will become your road map to success. Following through on this simple task today is the first step on your journey to success.

For the past twenty-four years, I have studied success and human nature, with a major focus on addiction and recovery. I have witnessed the horror of active addiction and the emotional trauma of relapse. I've also seen scores of addicts get sober yet not be able to experience all the joy and abundance of a full recovery. They continue to struggle in their relationships and suffer the burdens of financial insecurity.

I have helped many individuals experience a full recovery, and I now want to help you do the same. It is widely accepted that a good coach, mentor, or teacher is of great value in learning any skill. The ability of one recovering person to help another recovering person overcome addiction has been well documented. The practice of mentoring and sponsorship has proven itself through the successful rehabilitation of millions of suffering addicts and alcoholics. A good mentor saves valuable time and energy. I will endeavor to mentor you on your quest to create a personal action plan for life beyond sobriety. Let my experiences of both success and disappointment help hasten the journey to abundance you have embarked upon.

You may have noticed that I speak of God or the Creator throughout the introduction of this book. Just to clarify, I am not preaching or suggesting that you trade in your own personal concept of a higher power for mine or anyone else's. There are universally accepted truths that I present, and it is of little consequence if they come from the Bible, a scientist, a statesman, or a philosopher. This book is designed to produce action, create momentum, and achieve results, all while staying spiritually grounded, morally fit, and sober. For if you stay spiritually grounded and keep moving forward, you will never relapse. Many techniques for becoming successful will be discussed, but unless they are built on the bedrock of time-tested moral values, any profit you gain will be short-lived.

The only way to maintain your sobriety and move beyond it to enjoy a full recovery is to start by building a solid moral foundation.

So I ask you now: Are you sober? What's next? Once you achieve sobriety, what do you dream of accomplishing? What is your potential? What gifts and abilities has the Creator given you? The power to be a miracle is in you. Be an expression of who you really are, and you will be blessed. You will live without fear. You will live your true potential. The world is full of miracles, as I've experienced in my own life and as we saw in

Dr. Ted's story. We witness the miracle of full recovery every day. By witnessing, demonstrating, and sharing with others, we learn to abandon our belief in lack and deprivation in favor of belief in joy and abundance.

Let me welcome you to a life of abundance. I am glad you have decided you are worthy of the best life has to offer. We've been expecting you. Welcome to Full Recovery.

PART I

EXPLORATION

Open Your Mind

The world we have created is a product of our thinking;
it cannot be changed without changing our thinking.
—ALBERT EINSTEIN

ALL OF US ARE AWARE of people who started with the most humble, unremarkable, or average beginnings, yet still managed to soar to great heights. People who were able to move beyond the economic or societal labels that were thrust upon them and instead decided to follow their dreams. Eric Clapton is an example of such a person.

Eric Clapton entered this world as the son of an unwed teenage mother. His father was a soldier who abandoned them and returned to his home in Canada after his tour of duty. Eric was raised by his grandmother and her second husband, whom he was led to believe were his parents. He was given a guitar at age thirteen and struggled to learn how to play it. He found it so difficult he often considered quitting, but his deeply rooted love of music helped him develop the perseverance needed to continue trying.

Clapton went to college but failed out after one year. He then became a manual laborer, but his love of the blues kept drawing him back to music. In the early 1960s, he started playing for free at London clubs in between the set breaks of the headlining bands. He decided to make a commitment to music and eventually was discovered.

What did he do next? What everyone with an addictive personality usually does: he started to self-sabotage. He began drinking and drugging to excess. He became a heroin addict. He fought with other band members. He had volatile relationships with women. When it all became too much, he withdrew from the world and stayed isolated for years in a drug-induced state of depression. Although Clapton had enjoyed professional success, his demons kept him from truly benefiting from that success. Finally, after decades of depression and addiction, he hit bottom and did what he needed to do to get sober.

In 1993, he started discussing the possibility of opening a world-class center for the treatment of addiction, and by 1998 he had turned it into reality.

I once heard an interview with Clapton during which someone suggested that it was easier for him to stay sober because of all the money and success he had achieved. Clapton responded that, to the contrary, he was the perfect example that money and fame don't equal happiness. He went on to say he had every material thing a person could want, yet considered suicide daily until he got sober. He considers the years he has spent in sobriety the happiest and most productive of his life. He is a survivor and a great example of turning adversity into opportunity. He has used his personal challenges to inspire others through both his music and his treatment center.

As alcoholics and addicts, we sometimes feel we have been dealt a bad hand that gives us an excuse to wallow in self-pity. "If you had my life, you'd drink too" is an all too familiar comment made by active alcoholics. All people experience adversity whether they are addicts or not. It's how you react to adversity that will determine the measure of fullness in your recovery.

Did you know that Thomas Edison was thrown out of school at an early age because the teacher believed he wasn't capable of learning? Albert Einstein didn't speak until he was three years old and his family nicknamed him "the slow one." As a young man, Abraham Lincoln failed at every career he attempted: as a businessman he was simply inadequate; as an engineer he performed so poorly he had to declare bankruptcy and the sheriff was forced to sell his surveying equipment to make restitution to his creditors.

It's how you react to adversity that will determine the measure of fullness in your recovery.

Lincoln, like many people, also suffered from depression and even fought suicidal tendencies throughout his life. Upon reflecting on this painful issue, he came up with one of his most famous quotes: "Most folks are about as happy as they make up their minds to be." Lincoln chose to focus on being happy rather than depressed. He is an excellent example of the power to be found in controlling your focus. His perseverance in the face of overwhelming odds has placed him in the company of some of the greatest political leaders and statesmen of all time. Abraham Lincoln's courage in the face of adversity not only abolished slavery but also preserved the United States as we know it.

I am not suggesting that you are the next Clapton, Edison, Einstein, or Lincoln—although you might be. Nor am I suggesting that there will be no detours, speed bumps, or stop signs along the road to full recovery. What I am saying is that every adversity is just another opportunity. Adversity is what propels human development. When faced with a challenge, you can choose where you want to direct your focus and how to respond to the situation.

Your Mind Is Your Personal Supercomputer

Your mind, therefore, is one of your most powerful recovery tools. Physically, human beings are weak. Our strength lies in our ability to think. It is our superior mind rather than our physical prowess that has allowed us to become the dominant life force on the planet. At one time, Neanderthals coexisted with the ancestors of modern humans. Neanderthals were physically much stronger but mentally much weaker than our ancestors. That is why Neanderthals have disappeared from the earth, but we *Homo sapiens* survive and thrive.

When challenged with the overwhelming severity of winter, the need for warmth pushed primitive mankind to develop the ability to control fire, make clothing, and build housing. In search of food, trade, and a better life, humankind needed to travel, which led to the creation of ships, automobiles, and planes. Out of fear of our own barbarism and selfishness evolved the human desire to live in harmony with one another. This led to the creation of governments and educational systems.

Adversity and frustration foster creative thinking—if you let them. Why is it that we fear adversity when we have so much evidence as to its long-term benefits for human development? The short answer is the ego, or in spiritual terms, the "false self."

From an early age, we are conditioned to associate adversity with pain. Your ego, or the false self, develops the habit of conforming rather than seeking radical solutions or exploring new ideas because what if they don't succeed? It becomes easier and less painful to the ego to not take action rather than to take action and face the possibility of failing.

Your perceived problems are actually enormous opportunities for growth in disguise. In reality, failure and success are nothing more than a matter of perception.

When faced with adversity, search out creative solutions that could help you advance or even open new doors you may have never discovered otherwise. Don't get too hung up or worried about the perceived problems in your life. As soon as you solve one problem, you'll start looking around for a new one to solve. That's how we humans behave. It's a characteristic of our species.

If you are fully committed to reaching your potential, then setbacks are just the training you need for getting there. Welcome adversity because it encourages you to use your mind to overcome the problem. Your mind is a powerful supercomputer that has the ability to solve practically any problem. You simply need to ask it the right question. As the saying goes, "garbage in, garbage out." This is why it is so important to learn to master this powerful tool. Every time you use your mind, you learn to do more with that tool. Mind-altering chemicals short-circuit your computer. It's like introducing a virus into your software.

Substitute Faith for Hope

The next principle you need to understand is the importance of substituting faith for hope. Most people hope that their lives will get better, but most people aren't achieving the results they hope for. Hope is merely a beginning. Hope is waiting for something to happen in the future. Faith is the realization that things are already happening right now. You need to move from hope to faith.

> Faith is strong.
>
> Faith is emotional.
>
> Faith is inspirational.
>
> Faith creates a sense of certainty so powerful that it allows us to believe—beyond any rational argument—in someone, in something, or in a particular outcome.
>
> Faith is the belief in an unseen force that creates results that are manifested in the material world.

The Bible says that faith can move mountains . . . but it doesn't tell you to bring a shovel and lunch. You will need to take your faith and combine it with action; both are required in order to turn your dreams into reality.

The truths I have presented in this book are worthy of your faith. They have worked for me and countless others. They will work for you if take action and implement them in your life.

You Are the Mirror of What You Do

Another truth deserving of your faith is the principle that we are all mirror reflections of what we show the world. This principle has been recognized by all civilizations since ancient times. In the West, it is referred to as the law of reciprocity. In the East, it is referred to as karma. Jesus summed it up when he told us, "As you sow, so shall you reap." Nineteenth-century American Transcendentalist Ralph Waldo Emerson stated it this way in his essay "The Law of Compensation": "Every act rewards itself . . ." Sixteenth-century English physicist and mathematician Isaac Newton observed in nature that for every action there is an equal and opposite reaction. His third law of motion shows that this principle affects *everything* in the universe, not just human beings.

If you give fear, hate, or anger to another, it will encourage them to respond in kind. If you gossip or speak ill of another, you will attract the same qualities to yourself. Even if someone does not speak ill of you, your guilty conscience will convince you that people are gossiping about you. If you are instinctively mean to others, people will treat you with meanness. If you want to be a leader and decide to lead through intimidation and fear, you may succeed temporarily, but eventually people will revolt. If you're strong enough to crush the revolt, then people will run from you. The ones who don't run will be weak and not worthy of associating with anyway.

It is these types of undisciplined behaviors that inspire the same behavior in others.

If you hold your hand over a flame, it will burn you every time, not just some of the time. The same holds true for the principle that you are a mirror of all things you give. Whatever you show the world will always reflect back to you. Why don't you just accept this as true?

We see the fruitlessness of trying to cheat this law play out everywhere we look, from the classroom to the boardroom to the world stage. Thousands of years of turmoil and war in the Middle East are a perfect example of the results you get when you try to cheat the law. For centuries the region has been a mirror image of religious, ego-driven, fear-based conduct carried out on a national level. The national ego says we are right so you are wrong. Our God is right and yours is wrong. All sides claim the distinction of being directed by God and divinely inspired. Each side attacks and counterattacks. It solves nothing and depletes everyone. Each side receives what they give.

Now, I'm not saying that you should accept mistreatment from anyone. I am also assuming that sometimes people have not always treated you well and that life has not always been fair to you. What I am suggesting is that you have a choice regarding how you act and react.

Life Is Not Fair; Be Grateful

We may act justly toward one person yet watch as that person acts unjustly toward us and appears to benefit by his actions. Looks can be deceiving. This example leads to the next truth I want to discuss: Life is not fair. I have learned to have gratitude every day that life is not fair. Is it fair that people are born with disabilities and diseases and I was not? Is it fair that in the past I smoked cigarettes, yet I don't have cancer and others do? Is it fair that I was born in America, the world's wealthiest nation, and someone else was born in Somalia and is starving? Is it fair that many died drinking and drugging, and I did not? I thank God daily that life is not fair.

All of us can make our own list if we think about it. An

example might be, how many times did you break the law by purchasing illegal drugs or driving under the influence versus how many times were you caught? The idea is to start focusing on the gifts you have been given. Be grateful that you have been granted another day of life. If any of us received the fullness of karmic justice, we'd be dead or in jail. We have received the gift of grace, which has saved us from the full weight of our actions. Recognize this fact and stop making excuses.

Fair has nothing to do with anything. We all must play the hand we're dealt.

Ann's Journey to Full Recovery

How would you like to have been dealt this hand? Ann is from a small fishing island located in the North Atlantic off the coast of Canada. Ann's birth was the result of her teenage mother being raped by a Chinese seaman. The island has a notorious reputation for untreated alcoholism and poverty.

Soon after she was born, Ann was removed from her mother by a Christian organization and placed in an orphanage. One of her siblings was already living there, along with many other children the religious organization had deemed at risk. One day a couple from the United States arrived at the orphanage and adopted Ann's sibling. Ann was left behind. Over the next few years, children kept being adopted, but no one seemed to want Ann.

Several years after they adopted Ann's brother, the American couple returned for Ann. But when they arrived at the border, she was denied entry into the United States because the laws had changed. Ann was sent back to the orphanage. Following still more years of legal battles, Ann's adoptive parents were finally able to bring her to their home in New Jersey, and Ann was reunited with her brother.

I think you'll agree that Ann's childhood was filled with more adversity and unfairness than most of us have had to endure. But rather than a happy ending, things only got tougher. Ann found it difficult to relate to her new surroundings. She had no point of reference as to how to socialize with children in her metropolitan community, given her sheltered upbringing on an island. She looked different and felt different.

She was placed in a parochial school where her differences became more pronounced. Although Ann was very intelligent and the education provided by the school was exceptional, it was not a good fit for either. Ann was a creative and imaginative child, and these qualities were considered undesirable in the rigid educational structure in which she found herself. This only added to her low self-esteem issues. She felt as though she didn't fit in. Next Ann experienced a trauma of epic proportions. A family member of her adoptive parents raped her.

The unending and unfair saga that was Ann's life finally became too much for her, and she sought escape through self-medicating. She just didn't want to feel anymore. Ann became an alcoholic and drug addict. This form of escape worked only temporarily, of course, because now she had all the new problems that develop from a life of addiction.

I met Ann sixteen years ago when I was experiencing an extremely low point in my own recovery. I had spent years climbing the corporate ladder and was used to compounding my successes one on top of the other. My ego was in overdrive and my future looked bright. Then, as it sometimes does, life had another idea about which direction I should be heading.

My situation was this: the company I worked for was in transition. I was a top producer in my company, and I assumed that because of this my job was secure. It turned out my thought process was flawed. The new leadership had other ideas about where I should be working. I found myself caught in the midst of a Machiavellian power struggle.

I was overextended in my finances. I had just built the house of my dreams and had enrolled my son in an expensive private college.

The pressure kept building. My physical and mental health worsened, yet I would not slow down. The drive to achieve, what at the time I considered success, became paramount over everything else in life and I lost all perspective. Then the bottom fell out. Years earlier, before I got sober, I was involved in one particularly nasty motorcycle accident where I suffered a broken back. Because of several broken vertebrae that never healed properly and the pressure being placed on my spinal cord, I developed a debilitating paralysis in my leg and could not walk. I underwent spinal surgery that kept me bedridden for months. My family life was also strained as my wife and I went through the grieving that accompanied her father's slip into darkness as he experienced the final phases of Alzheimer's disease.

To sum it up, I found myself facing career, financial, health, and family trouble. It was one of those life-changing moments. What would I do? Would I run? Would I fight? Would I drink? I decided it was time to take action and refocus on my recovery. That's when Ann appeared.

Ann was trying to get sober after twenty-five years of hardcore addiction. I devoted my free time to helping her, and other newcomers seeking to get sober, learn about recovery. Helping others was great for me because when I was helping someone else, I was not thinking about my own problems.

It was time well spent. As I forgot about my problems, I started to focus on solutions. I asked myself better questions—such as, "What lessons am I supposed to be learning from my present challenges?"—and received better answers. Through the process of working with people like Ann, I realized the joy that comes from helping others. I developed an attitude of gratitude. Suddenly my problems didn't seem so bad. I began a major paradigm shift in my perceptions of success. Even my reading habits changed. Where I once focused on reading books about success and money, I found myself seeking deeper truths and spiritual solutions to problems in the material world.

It was during this time that I decided I would like to chart a new career path. Although bedridden and in much pain, I made a conscious decision to avoid painkillers. I chose to distract myself by focusing my attention on designing a new life rather than dulling my senses. I was not able to walk, but I could use my mind, my supercomputer. I had always been interested in real estate, so I began reading books and familiarizing myself with the market. I had no job and little savings but had a gut feeling this was what I should be doing, so I took action. The timing was perfect. It was 1998 and the real estate boom was just beginning. The first home I bought was a corporate-owned property. I learned six months after purchasing the vacant house that Ann had been the last tenant to occupy the space prior to my purchasing it. It's just another example of how lives intersect and that God has a sense of humor. I don't believe in coincidences, but I do believe in divine appointment. The universe unfolds as it should.

I have been blessed to witness Ann's recovery. She got sober and developed a plan of action for moving beyond it by following the suggestions in this book. From a fearful, desperate soul has grown a woman of poise and grace. Ann has had her challenges and setbacks along the path to full recovery but she has never given up. At one point she fell victim to the false belief that because a doctor prescribed mood-altering drugs, they were OK for her to take. As addicts, our minds and bodies do not discriminate between legal and illegal drugs. Ann never gave up and is clean and sober today. She uses her experiences to help other women who are seeking a better life. She met and married a great guy who loves and appreciates her as a wife and mother of their son. Ann has embraced the ideas I describe in *Full Recovery* and is constantly challenging herself to reach her full potential.

Adversity propels human development.

Meeting Ann at that difficult time in my own recovery didn't happen by chance. I would never have chosen any of the challenges I was presented with. But by accepting God's will for me, I was able to make distinctions that led me to a higher consciousness. I discovered the peace that comes from gratitude. It was an example of my higher power leading me to the right path. I just had to be willing to trust in God and stay true to my principles. With every adversity there comes an opportunity. Adversity propels human development.

When things don't work out fairly, which usually means to our benefit, we must continue having faith in the principles we know to be true. The benefit or punishment we deserve rarely comes from where it should. But come it will. Every act rewards itself.

When you are reading through the chapters in this book and completing the lessons, remember the mirror:

If you want to enjoy a full recovery, help others to recover.

If you want to be loved, give love.

If you want to be wealthy, help others to achieve wealth.

The same goes for anything else you want.

The Lord's Prayer says, "Forgive us our trespasses as we forgive those who trespass against us." It doesn't say forgive me my trespasses and I'll think about forgiving someone else's. It says as I forgive only then will I be forgiven. This is an unbreakable law.

First You Do the Work, Then You Receive the Benefit

People believe you are successful because you earn a lot of money, when just the opposite is true. You earn a lot of money because you are successful. Take professional athletes, for example. From the time they are small children, they play and strive to be the best. Through elementary school, high school, and college, they practice and persevere. They are already successful before they see the big paydays as a pro. The same holds true for anyone who is living the successful life he or she has chosen, whether it's as a doctor, a musician, an artist, or any number of professions.

First you must do the work, and then you receive the benefit. Any other way would be contrary to common sense. It would be like trying to drive your car before adding the gas. You must first add the fuel and then receive the benefit. How many people experience lack, suffer disappointment, and live in mediocrity because they won't embrace this simple reality: there is no such thing as a free lunch.

⁂

To some, the ideas I spelled out in this chapter may seem radical or strange. Please don't let that discourage you. Unfamiliarity can cause apprehension. Keep an open mind and try not to be too contemptuous about investigating this new way of thinking. Ask yourself if you are getting the results you want from your current beliefs. Ask yourself if you are living the lifestyle you want. Ask yourself if you are achieving the results you expect. If you are not, the thoughts and beliefs you are holding on to need to be examined. Take it on faith, gather up some emotion, and get ready to receive abundantly. Get ready to know yourself.

Let's Review

- Your mind is your supercomputer and a powerful recovery tool.
- Adversity is often an opportunity.
- Substitute faith for hope.
- You are the mirror of what you do.
- Life is not fair. Be grateful.
- You must do the work before you receive the reward.

FULL RECOVERY ACTION PLAN EXERCISES

This chapter began by asking you to open your mind. Your mind is a powerful tool; let's learn to use it. Take out your Full Recovery Action Plan and answer the following questions:

1. Write down one instance in which you were able to overcome adversity. Keep in mind there are many ways to overcome obstacles. In a sports competition, for instance, it can be through practice and determination. In recovering from addiction, it can be through surrender by admitting your powerlessness over addiction and turning it over to a higher power. In business, it can be through creativity and drive. Open your mind.

2. Now, write down one challenge you are currently facing and find the opportunity in the adversity. Maybe you are struggling in recovery, which is why you are seeking help and answers in this book. Perhaps you have lost a job, which is a perfect time to question your career path and could possibly lead you in a new direction. Maybe you are experiencing a family crisis that can open the door to developing a deeper and more abiding faith. Remember: adversity propels human development.

3. Write down one of your undisciplined behaviors that you would like to change. Keep in mind that the mirror always reflects back to you. Do you hold a grudge against someone? Do you enjoy participating in gossip and other forms of character assassination? Is procrastination or your inability to take action really masking a more deeply rooted fear?

4. Write down at least one thing you experienced today for which you are grateful. Do you enjoy good health? Are you loved? Are you sober today? Gratitude helps you to understand what you want, what you enjoy, and what brings you true contentment.

Know Yourself

Man, know thyself, and thou wilt know the universe and the Gods.
—PYTHAGORAS

THIS INSCRIPTION WAS CARVED in stone at the entrance to the temple of Apollo at Delphi in ancient Greece. Hundreds of years before the birth of Christ, philosophers such as Socrates, Plato, and Aristotle tried to understand man and his place in the cosmos. These curious observers of human nature pondered many of the same questions and challenges we face today. They warned against the dangers of blind obedience to authority. They valued education, self-expression, and personal freedom.

The Roman philosopher Seneca marveled at man's self-destructive tendencies in his observation, "Drunkenness is voluntary madness."

These early philosophers pursued the truth about the nature of humankind and the world we inhabit. They tried to develop a concept of God that would explain the existence of all that exists. This illustrates that although we live in a more technologically advanced era than these men, human nature and the quest for truth remains the same. Truth is the highest reality.

The Value of Knowing Who You Are

How, exactly, are you to know yourself, and why is this process necessary?

I would like to address the second part of that question first. If you have been involved in a twelve-step program, you are familiar with the concept of taking a moral inventory. And if you are sober, you have probably at least begun the process of examining your life. The purpose of using this time-proven method in recovery programs is to take a retrospective look at the character flaws that parallel addiction. It's a way to discover and correct glaring personality traits that can stand in the way of recovery and possibly lead to relapse. It is my experience that people unwilling to do this exercise have little chance of long-term recovery, which, of course, is the foundation of successful living. This type of moral inventory involves questioning your motives and deals mainly with the inappropriate actions you took while in active addiction and the effect these actions had on yourself and others.

The problem I have observed is that although many people are able to get sober or live in recovery, in part, from taking a moral inventory, they are not able to achieve the same outstanding results in other areas of their lives. Many are still struggling financially, as well as in their family and personal relationships. Others aren't able to hold on to a working spirituality. These real-life problems place unnecessary strain on the recovering person and are often contributing factors to relapse.

As I witnessed this phenomenon, I started to ask myself better questions. The realization came to me that if my moral beliefs needed examination, then my most basic values and core beliefs regarding life also needed to be scrutinized. By delving even deeper, beyond a moral inventory alone, I gained a more complete understanding of who I was at that time. More important, I uncovered aspects of my self-imposed rulebook that were no longer serving me well.

All businesses take inventory. And no business of any noteworthy success would do an inventory without documenting the results. This allows management to look for patterns and make judgments about how to increase the business's effectiveness, efficiency, and profitability.

In this book, I am speaking about the business of life . . . your life. To make your life more profitable, a thorough inventory of your assets and liabilities must be done.

> Many people are able to get sober or live in recovery from taking a moral inventory, but they are not able to achieve the same outstanding results in other areas of their lives.

To become successful and experience a full recovery, you must be willing to see yourself as you truly are, to look deeper into yourself than you have before. The ability to separate your talents and assets from your fantasies and defects is the beginning of your journey toward abundance.

The idea is to develop your assets and overcome your deficiencies. To accomplish this feat takes a fearless self-examination. As Socrates put it, "The unexamined life is not worth living."

For many, this can be a frustrating or even fearful proposition. Most people dare not look too deeply into their hearts for fear of what they might find. It is said that you can only be as honest as you are aware. The reason for this exercise is to become aware of the misguided belief systems that stop you from pursuing the life you were created to enjoy.

The catch is that with awareness comes responsibility. You will no longer be able to hide behind ignorance.

The answer, then, to the first part of the question I asked earlier—"How, exactly, are you to know yourself?"—is quite simple, but it isn't easy. It is as simple as asking yourself the right questions. Our unique ability to ask questions is the key to gaining knowledge. From ancient times to our modern technological age, all advancement has been tied to the quality of our questioning. Likewise, your advancement will be tied to the quality of your questioning, as well as to the fearlessness and honesty of your answers.

The first question I asked myself was, "How am I staying sober?" The answer was, "By imitating and following suggestions from people who know how to get and stay sober."

The next question was, "Can this philosophy work in other areas of my life?" The answer was, "Yes."

What I quickly learned was that one question usually leads to another. For example, asking myself, "How do I seek out someone who is getting the results I want if I don't know what I want?" led to the follow-up question, "If I don't know what I want, how can I define my idea of success?"

What I also soon discovered, though, is that it is easy to start going around in endless circles of questioning and still not get any closer to the goal of self-discovery. This is why it's important for you to answer the questions I present in this book in the order that I've placed them in the chapters. Concern yourself only with the given chapter you are working on at any one moment. Try not to let your mind wander into unrelated areas; instead, focus on the question at hand and the chapter content related to it. Keep your focus, and you will achieve a more desirable outcome.

Understanding Who You Are

As you get into this process of uncovering your true beliefs, it's important to keep in mind that the Creator has given humans a few special gifts, reserved for us alone. One of these gifts is the power of choice. All other creatures live by instinct. Human beings are the only one of God's creatures afforded the right to choose the actions they will take. Unfortunately, we often exercise this right concerning the most trivial choices, such as what to eat or what clothes to wear. Too often, less preference is given to the more significant choices, such as what career path to follow or what type of higher power to acknowledge. These important decisions are relegated to someone else, quite often our parents, church, or government.

You are experiencing your current reality because of the choices you have made and the choices you continue to make on a regular basis. This is a bitter pill to swallow, but it must be swallowed if you want a full recovery. It is *your choice* to live in ignorance or to bravely press forward and discover the Creator's purpose for you.

The first step in gaining a better understanding of who you are is asking yourself where your beliefs originated. Did you choose them consciously? How do you know they are correct?

I asked myself these and many other questions, and I was surprised by the answers. Let me share some of my own process of discovery with you.

When I began this process, I was in early recovery and my ideas were still quite warped. At that time, I believed a man talked tough and acted tougher. He had to be completely independent and self-reliant. I considered it perfectly acceptable to be high 24/7. I believed you should be feared so as not to be double-crossed. Retaliation should be swift and overwhelming. Take what you want today because tomorrow might never come. Eat, drink, and be merry, for tomorrow we die. The challenge became, of course, that I didn't die. I lived.

Life during early sobriety, with this misguided belief system lingering in my mind, became increasingly difficult, and it was a confusing time for me. There were no pink clouds or any sense of relief like I have heard others have experienced. I was angry. I didn't want to drink or drug, but my ego and habitual ways of thinking kept presenting formidable barriers that were becoming increasingly difficult to overcome. I was abstaining from all mind-altering chemicals, but I was far from sober.

Addiction for me was always a disease of "not enough." I wasn't good enough, smart enough, or talented enough. These insecurities morphed into there's not enough booze, sex, drugs, or money. I craved "more" to fill the void inside me. Too much of everything was never enough. Recovery was beginning to present the same problems. I soon realized that abstinence alone would not be enough.

Around this time a close friend, with some good sobriety and who had observed my frustration, suggested that I write down my life story. He thought it might help me figure out what was holding me back. I spent the next several weeks writing down my history and reviewing my actions. This process gave me many insights. I realized, after much thought and soul searching, that I had not chosen most of my beliefs intelligently. Most weren't even chosen consciously.

We live in a world full of people trying to get our attention. It starts with our parents but also includes friends, teachers, television, advertisers—the list goes on ad infinitum. I began to realize that many of the major beliefs I held about God, money, success, happiness, and life in general were hand-me-downs from someone else . . . but whom? I wrote down my family and personal history and tried to figure out where it all started and how these beliefs came to be.

When I had completed the process, I burned the copy of my life story but kept the list of questions that it prompted. I was learning to use my mind, my supercomputer. To this day, whenever the old negative movie starts playing in my head, I substitute the image of my old life going up in flames and consciously turn my focus back to the present. By analyzing my life, I had developed better questions to ask myself, which led to more productive answers.

To create a new future and abandon addiction, I had to first understand the past and then unburden myself from it. As I examined my beliefs and my rules for living, I realized that I really hadn't chosen many of them; rather, I had simply accepted them. What I mean by this is that many of my beliefs were learned behaviors. They became part of my

> I made the decision to live addiction free, and the foundation of my new life is built on the bedrock belief that I will live in recovery one day at a time.

personality through suggestion and repetition. Some were just absorbed along the way when I was in a receptive state.

Having gone through the process of questioning my own rules for living, I discovered that my mentors and old ideas of success didn't serve me well. I decided to change course and thus my destiny.

I embraced the fact that I'm an adult capable of choosing what I want to believe and what rules I'm willing to let influence my life. I made the decision to live addiction free, and the foundation of my new life is built on the bedrock belief that I will live in recovery one day at a time.

Remember this: If you believe you can or you can't do something, you are right. It's your choice to believe in addiction, resentment, and limitation or to courageously press forward and experience a full recovery. For you to expand beyond your present situation, you must develop the fearlessness needed to challenge the beliefs your ego embraces. These beliefs are not the real you. They are the misguided veils of illusion the ego hides behind.

Let's Review

- Misguided beliefs lead to poor results.
- You can abandon beliefs that are no longer serving you well.
- Ask better questions and you will receive better answers.
- You get to choose your beliefs, so choose wisely—intelligently and consciously.
- If you believe you can or you can't accomplish a task . . . you are right.

FULL RECOVERY ACTION PLAN EXERCISES

Assuming you have the willingness to indulge in an unvarnished self-examination, it's time to get to know yourself. It's time to discover how you became you, and if this is who you want to be. The following list of questions is by far the longest in this book. These are the questions I asked myself that jump-started my quest for a full recovery. Don't wait, get started and make sure you answer them all. This process of discovery is the foundation on which your new life will be built. As Plato put it, "Self-conquest is the greatest of victories."

Take out your Full Recovery Action Plan and answer the following questions:

1. List the people and organizations who have had the greatest influence on you.
2. Are the people or organizations that influenced you currently enjoying the success, peace of mind, and abundance you hope to achieve?
3. Is your current outlook and/or belief system hindering or helping you achieve an abundant lifestyle?
4. Do you believe you can overcome your addiction?
5. Are you 100 percent committed to living addiction free?
6. What are you afraid of? Make a detailed list.
7. How and when did these fears come to originate?
8. Are you willing to take the necessary actions to conquer fear?

9. What types of situations cause you anxiety?
10. Who do you resent? Why do you resent them?
11. Why are you not willing to forgive them?
12. Who do you envy? Why do you envy them?
13. What is your attitude toward work? Fill in the blank: Work is ______________________________.
14. Are you happy in your present career?
15. What is your definition of success?
16. How much money do you want?
17. Do you have a game plan for earning that amount?
18. What are your feelings about money? Fill in the blank: Money is ______________________________.
19. Do you believe you are or could be successful? Why?
20. Who do you admire? What about them do you admire?
21. Do you have goals? Are they written down? If not, take time to write four goals now.
22. How much time each day do you spend working on your goals?
23. What skills do you need to develop to reach your goals?
24. What's holding you back from acquiring these skills?
25. What's your reaction when someone says that you *can't* accomplish something?

26. How do you respond when someone offends you or treats you poorly?
27. Do you enjoy people?
28. Do you trust people? Fill in the blank: People are ________________________________.
29. Who do you love?
30. Who loves you?
31. What is your definition of love? Is it freely given or must it be earned?
32. What type of Creator or higher power do you believe in?
33. What characteristics does this being possess?
34. How did you arrive at this concept of God?
35. Does this concept of God serve you well?
36. What do you believe is the reason you were created?
37. What do you enjoy doing?
38. What special gifts or talents do you already possess?
39. Where do you see yourself living and working during the next five years and beyond?
40. What would you attempt if you knew you couldn't fail?
41. Who is the most important person alive today?

This last question is a no-brainer. For the purposes of your full recovery, the answer is you. There are many other questions that you can ask yourself, but if you have taken the time and done some soul searching, at this point you have a good overview of your current understanding of reality and what you value. This is a great starting point on your journey to unlocking your full potential! Now let's figure out what's been holding you back.

Fear

It is not death that a man should fear, but he should fear never beginning to live.
—MARCUS AURELIUS

DID YOU NOTICE any patterns as you reviewed your life history and examined who you THINK you really are? If you didn't, you probably haven't looked deep enough. If you did, and you are honest enough to break down all of your limiting beliefs, resentments, and character defects to the lowest common denominator, they can be summed up in one word: fear.

Fear of taking risk

Fear of being wrong

Fear of change

Fear of failure

Fear of success

Fear that there is not enough to go around

Fear of not getting what you think you deserve

Fear is an instinct designed to keep you safe in situations of perceived danger. This instinct causes an immediate reaction known as fight or flight. Whenever your safety is threatened, you either instinctively run away or stay and fight. Sometimes you do a combination of both, but either way, it is an automatic response to an outside stimulus.

Fear is also an intense and unpleasant emotion that is often caused by the anticipation of events that have not yet taken place. You run into problems when you let this one emotion be the principal guiding force in your life.

There is an insidious quality to fear that allows it to reproduce itself like a virus. It gets passed from person to person and, as a result, has a gradual and cumulative effect. We are assaulted daily with fearful suggestions. The media does its best to convince us that we are doomed. We are supposed to worry about everything from the stock market collapsing to mass extinction from a meteor striking our planet. We watch television and read newspapers unaware of the damaging effect they can have on our subconscious mind when we unconsciously accept these messages without questioning them.

Living in fear is seductive and habit-forming. It is as addictive as any drug; and much like drug addiction, it develops so subtly that it is well established before it becomes apparent.

Living in fear is seductive and habit-forming. It is as addictive as any drug; and much like drug addiction, it develops so subtly that it is well established before it becomes apparent.

When you live in the past, it is because of fear. Even if the past was painful or unpleasant, at least you know what happened. This can be less stressful than living in the present or with the uncertainty of the future. You fear the unknown. You fear physical and emotional pain and it keeps you from taking the types of actions that will bring you true happiness and peace of mind. The past is dead, and as Jesus told us, "Let the dead bury their dead."

No matter how hard you try, you cannot change the past. You can only change the now, this moment, which in turn will give you a different future.

The questions you answered at the end of the preceding chapter were designed to help you search out the truth about yourself. This is a necessary character-building exercise that must be done if you are going to proceed down the road of happiness unencumbered by the weight of your past.

Many people achieve the miracle of recovery from all sorts of addictions, yet they are still not able to demonstrate the same types of successes in other areas of their lives. I believe part of the reason for this is that they refuse to relinquish some of their old ideas. They go far enough to overcome addiction, but not any further. They question their beliefs and habits as far as their addiction is concerned, but they don't take the same open-minded approach to all other areas of their lives.

You may have noticed that I use the phrase "miracle of recovery." This phrase is often heard in recovery programs and implies an extraordinary event via divine intervention. If recovery from addiction truly is a miracle, which I believe it is, then this miracle can be taught, learned, and duplicated. If miracles are the cause of recovery from addiction, they can also be used to overcome any other difficulty. Your willingness to believe in miracles will result in a miraculous life.

Are you seeking a miraculous life beyond sobriety? Is your present reality one of overwhelming prosperity and fulfillment? Or is the fear of failure or the fear of change keeping you tethered to a mediocre existence?

If you are seeking to become better off financially or to build better-quality personal relationships, start letting go of the past. Your unworkable beliefs must be challenged and eradicated if you are going to enjoy success and freedom. All life takes place in the now, this moment. A successful life is built upon your ability to be in harmony with the present over an extended period of time. Living in the present is a choice.

The idea is not to live in the past mentally, replaying old mistakes and dramatizing poor decisions. Every time you revisit these mistakes, you experience them as freshly and intensely as when they happened. This is not productive. Whenever you live in the past, you steal from the present. You literally are throwing away the present moment.

The same concept holds true for living in the past even if you are replaying happier thoughts. Granted, this is much better than rehearsing fears and resentments, but it's an equal waste of time. It's much more rewarding to create new happiness and let go of the old.

Along the same line of thought, let's talk about resentments. Resentments are nothing more than fear and anger turned inward. You must get rid of this crippling emotion if you wish to experience peace of mind. When you hold on to a resentment or grudge, you relive the perceived injustice many times over, and it affects you at every level. Physically, the body tenses up, adrenaline spikes, and you feel achy and nauseous. Sometimes you become more emotionally upset than when the actual situation occurred. Not only is this disturbing to you, it is also a complete waste of time and effort.

You may feel justified in continuing this morbid and fruitless behavior, but the most you can hope to gain is more anger, fear, depression, and stagnation. Let's expel this junk once and for all and be done with it. You can't be filled up until you are emptied out. When you lose your anger and resentment, you can replace them with joy and freedom. Sounds like a pretty good deal, doesn't it?

When I first attempted to know myself, it was a scary proposition. There I was: sober for the first time in twenty years, yet with no reference points as how to live life on life's terms. For years I had run from frustration and adversity, and when I ran, I ran straight to the bottle. After having made the decision to live addiction free, I had to develop another way of dealing with the challenges of life. I had to overcome my fear of the present and the future if I was going to achieve full recovery.

You can't be filled up until you are emptied out. Lose your anger and resentment and replace them with joy and freedom.

This was not easy. I had spent a great deal of time reliving the past and justifying my reasons for doing so. But I could not move forward with one foot stuck in the past, so I had to let go completely.

An example of this was letting go of the resentment and ongoing prejudice I felt toward organized religion. My ego had convinced me that I deserved to hold a grudge against my former church and what I perceived as its hypocritical ways. I did not like being looked down upon or judged by their rules, but wasn't I guilty of the same behavior? Didn't I judge the church? Wasn't I also being hypocritical?

As long as I held resentment toward the church and its teachings, I was unable to clear my mind and allow the grace of God to enter. I was beating myself over the head with the same club of self-righteousness that the church had used on me. I had to develop a different point of reference if I was going to be able to experience any peace of mind and develop a working spirituality. Fear had convinced my ego that to challenge religion gave me some type of power and an air of superiority. Yet here I was, miserable and unable to demonstrate any type of power—not financially, not in my personal relationships, not with my quality of life, and not even with a joyful recovery. Yet my ego convinced me that I was right.

I needed to change. I chose to accept the fact that just because the rules of the church did not work for me didn't mean that they didn't work. The fact that millions of people are receiving strength and comfort from the Catholic Church is a testament to the validity of its teachings. Forgiving the church was the beginning of the process of forgiving myself. Removing my resentment allowed me to create some space in my mind to seek out a God of my understanding.

> Nothing has any meaning but the meaning you give it. Look for the lesson and the opportunity in every situation.

As you develop a healthy attitude toward fear, I would like you to think about this statement: Nothing has any meaning but the meaning you give it.

I discovered that I had a choice in how I responded to life situations. Just because I held certain beliefs in the past didn't mean that I had to be afraid of changing them today. Now when I'm frustrated or facing adversity, I look for the lesson and the opportunity in the situation. I consciously give it a different meaning, deriving a positive from what could be viewed as a potential negative. I choose how I will respond instead if simply reacting. The way you look at your current situation is also a choice.

I believe it's possible to convince yourself of just about anything—either negative or positive. For example, on the negative side, a drug abuser can convince himself that self-destruction is partying, or fun. An eighty-five-pound bulimic can convince herself that she is overweight. A sadist or a rapist can achieve sexual gratification through the abuse of himself or others.

You have probably heard of the Reverend Jim Jones and the horror that took place under his drug-crazed guidance in Guyana. Reverend Jim convinced himself that he was a man of God. However, when his authority was challenged, his ego demanded mass suicide and the execution of his own followers.

Let me give you an example from a real-life situation I witnessed. Around the same time I met Ann, a man approached me and asked I if would help him reach a full recovery. He was a large man with broad shoulders. He was heavily covered with tattoos and had a shaved head. He had done his best to appear as intimidating and as imposing as possible.

I began by asking him to tell me about himself. He explained that he was an opiate addict. He had been involved in an automobile accident as a child and was introduced to painkillers and hooked from the start. As a young boy, he had felt powerless being hospitalized for long stretches, and he sought out role models to help him feel empowered. He began to emulate the behavior of people who, through the eyes of a small boy, appeared to be confident and fearless. Bikers, rodeo cowboys, thugs, and womanizers drew his attention.

As I listened to him recount his story, I realized that as he had grown into adulthood, and addiction, he had fine-tuned this immature idea of manhood. The insecurities he had experienced as a young, addicted man with physical limitations led him to develop a delusional persona to deal with those insecurities and fears. His ego and addiction convinced him he was a tough guy and a ladies' man. He rode a Harley and became a competitive rodeo cowboy and a cheating spouse. Eventually, however, a forty-painkiller-a-day habit caught up with him and he wound up in rehab.

I told him about the same course of action I've outlined in this book. I explained that to enjoy a full recovery was a choice and it included developing better habits of thought. Nothing has any meaning but the meaning you give it. To abandon addiction and acquire abundance involved moving beyond the fear that the ego embraces.

After a relatively short period of time, it became apparent that this man was unwilling or incapable of the courage needed to push past his fears and change. Much of his false courage was derived from his addiction. For instance, when he was drug-free, he realized he was actually afraid of horses. This man who had competed in rodeos now wouldn't even mount a horse! He was a married man and a father of small children, but he was afraid to stop his womanizing ways. He was convinced that his wife might challenge his manhood if she thought he wasn't capable of getting other women. He needed to keep her in line. He was verbally abusive to his family and considered it an acceptable way to behave so his authority wouldn't be questioned.

I had to let him go. His tattoos and intimidating look were simply a mask worn by a man who was still a scared little boy hiding in plain sight. Unfortunately, he never realized that he was capable of overcoming fear by becoming willing to change.

These are extreme examples of self-justification, but they illustrate the truth that nothing has any meaning but the meaning you give it. The question I have for you is this: How often do you reinforce fear-based negative thinking in your own life through a poor inner dialogue? The truth is, we talk to ourselves all day long, and our conversations either underscore our fears or give us confidence.

You have a choice in how you talk to yourself. What type of conversations are you having?

> Do you reinforce fears that continue to hold you back?
>
> Do you tell yourself, "I don't know if I can succeed; the obstacles in front of me are too great, so why bother trying?"
>
> Do you ask yourself, "How come I never get a break?"
>
> Do you reinforce weak-minded thoughts? "Someday I'll fall in love; someday I'll make more money; someday I'll start my own business."
>
> Remember: *Today* is someday. Change the conversation!

If you are going to give meaning to your thoughts and allow them to direct your life, why not come up with some affirmations that serve your internal dialogue better? How much more fulfilling could your life be if you reinforced thoughts like these?

> I have been made by the Creator of the universe to be happy, creative, and successful.
>
> I have the ability to create the reality of my choosing.
>
> I am living abundantly today and every day hereafter.
>
> I am perfect in mind, body, and spirit.
>
> I can achieve all my goals.

This type of reinforcement is the first step toward overcoming your fears. This is an easy way of developing a new habit. After all, what is a habit but a learned behavior that is developed through repetition? Our habits become so automatic that we don't even think about them, we just act. Your limiting thoughts about yourself are nothing more than a bad habit. Living in fear is the same. It's time to develop some new, empowering habits and techniques. The time has come to overcome fear and negativity.

Overcoming Fear and Negativity

If I ask you what a fearful or defeated person looks like, what images come to mind? Your description would probably include adjectives such as anxious, uncomfortable, slumped shoulders, bowed head, downward gaze, shallow breathing, nervous. We all know the look. Some of us know it better than others because it's looking back at us in the mirror.

Now, along the same lines, how would you describe a successful, confident, motivated person? Images that come to mind are of someone who's energetic, erect, smiling, standing tall, shoulders back, head up, moving powerfully.

Our physiology on the outside is often a reflection of how we feel on the inside. What people seem to pay less attention to is the fact that this principle works both ways. How we carry ourselves on the outside can also have an enormous impact on how we feel on the inside.

How we carry ourselves on the outside can also have an enormous impact on how we feel on the inside.

One of the easiest ways to overcome fear and gain confidence is to simply change your physiology. Take a minute and try this little exercise.

Think, Feel, and Act Different

Think back to a time when everything went wrong. The person you wanted to date chose someone else or, worse, publicly humiliated you. Maybe you didn't make the team. Perhaps your husband or wife came home and told you they were leaving you for someone else. Maybe you lost your job or were informed of a serious health issue.

Focus on this memory intensely. Visualize it happening. Let your shoulders droop, lower your head, make your breathing shallow, and let your body go limp. Really feel as if it's happening right now. How do you feel?

My guess is not too well. At the very least, you probably don't feel motivated or empowered. More than likely you feel depressed, angry, or resentful. This is the kind of exercise that great majorities of people participate in every day. Is it any wonder why we seek distractions? Is it any wonder we self-medicate with a food, alcohol, drugs, and tobacco and then we feel guilty about being out of control and addicted, so we medicate some more and try to forget about that too? This is the endless cycle of addiction, depression, and remorse.

Let's develop a better habit. Clear your mind completely. Shake that feeling off. Stand up, throw your shoulders back, lift your head up, take a couple of deep breaths, and change your focus. Start thinking about a time when you were unbeatable, when everything you did turned out right. We all have had these moments. Maybe it was the day you were accepted into college or the day you received an A on a test. Think about the day you and your lover decided to get married or when you qualified for a new home. Think back to a time when you scored the winning goal or when your child was born. Remember the day you got a big promotion and a big fat raise. Really feel it, smile, be confident, walk around the room and enjoy that feeling of invincibility.

Notice the difference? Neither situation, negative or positive, has actually taken place in the last few minutes, but it didn't matter. Consciously moving your physical body in certain ways while changing your emotions and controlling what you allowed your mind to focus on enabled you to change the way you feel. When you feel different you act different.

When you change your physical stature and energy, the world treats you differently. There is a saying—move a muscle, change a thought—and if you did this exercise, you know it's true. When you feel down or fearful, you now know how to change that feeling instantly. Something as simple as picking your head up, moving with authority, or changing your breathing pattern can change the way you feel. The quicker you catch yourself drifting into fearfulness or negativity, the easier it will be to take action to turn it around.

In that last exercise we touched on rejection, which is a major fear for many people. A baseless fear of rejection keeps us from advancing at the level of our capabilities and from taking action.

Remember this: No one can make you feel rejected without your participation and acceptance.

Rather than fearing rejection and not taking action, ask yourself this question: "How defeated will I feel if I don't try; or how great will I feel when I conquer my fear and move ahead?"

Most successful people have learned to overcome massive amounts of rejection. It takes practice and perseverance to continue on when faced with adversity.

Everyone has come up against challenges or faced rude and obnoxious people. When someone treats me harshly, I remember what Buddha said we should ask ourselves: "If a man offers you a gift, and you refuse to accept the gift, who does the gift belong to?" In other words, if someone offers me rudeness or sarcasm, I don't accept the gift; I continue on my way. He can keep that gift for himself. If someone attempts to make me feel unwanted or inferior, I look at it logically and unemotionally. If this same person called me a billionaire would it make me one dollar richer? Do you see my point? Another person's opinion of me is irrelevant. My opinion of me is what counts.

One of the ways in which I learned to overcome fear, including my fear of rejection, was to write out some positive affirmations that I committed to memory. I needed to improve my opinion of myself. I was tired of the old negative recording in my head, so I started a practice that continues today. I kept one affirmation on each fingertip of my right hand, and one on each fingertip of my left hand. Here are the five I kept on my right hand at that time.

God wants me sober.

God wants me happy.

God wants me spiritually fit.

God wants me abundantly wealthy.

God wants me to help others.

I started my affirmations with the word *God* after reflecting on my life. As the fog of early recovery began to clear, I started to appreciate the gifts my higher power had given me. Prior to this awakening, my life was one of selfishness and addiction. This unworkable lifestyle culminated in physical, emotional, and mental pain. My affirmations not only reminded me of that fact but also gave me the leverage I needed to stay the course and recover.

My affirmations gave me a quick way of changing my focus when the old recording in my head started playing, but the reasons that I associated with these affirmations allowed me, over time, to reprogram my subconscious mind. The logic behind my affirmations was as follows:

I believe the architect of life wants me clearheaded, healthy in mind, body, and spirit.

—*God wants me sober.*

I believe I was created to be happy. I have found that happiness is not something to be chased after or purchased, but is the by-product of living a productive, creative, and giving life.

—*God wants me happy.*

My degree of spiritual fitness is in direct proportion to my ability to bring my desires into agreement with God's plan. My idea of spiritual fitness grows and changes as my understanding increases. It is in constant flux. I have also noticed that if I am not progressing forward, I start slipping backward.

—*God wants me spiritually fit.*

The Creator supplies all the abundance I shall ever need or want, not just material riches, but love, health, family, truth, intelligence, and peace of mind.

—*God wants me abundantly wealthy.*

Just as the Creator helps me, I must help others. Just as all the laws of nature are unbreakable, the law of reciprocity is constant and unchanging. If I want help, I must first give it. If I want abundance, I must give abundantly. To enjoy a full recovery, I must help others to recover. To become wealthy, I must help others to achieve wealth. If I seek forgiveness, I must first forgive.

—*God wants me to help others.*

I am not suggesting you need to start your affirmations with the word *God* unless you feel moved to do so. I am simply showing you an example of the process I used to rewrite the software in my mind. We have all heard of brainwashing. Well, my brain needed washing. By reprogramming the way I communicated with myself, I was able to accept the fact that my Creator equipped me with unlimited potential. Knowing that I am never alone and that my higher power is closer than my breath, has removed all doubt. By realizing that I am a miracle of creation, I can fearlessly press forward, fulfilling my destiny, earning the privilege of being alive. Understanding—and more important—accepting this fact was a major step in overcoming not only my fear but also my self-imposed limitations.

Fear keeps you from experiencing life to its fullest. It keeps you from giving of yourself and your wealth, as you should. You fear that there will not be enough left when you need it. You're afraid that people will take advantage of you and your generosity. In reality, just the opposite is true.

Remember the golden rule? Do to others whatever you would have them do to you. In reality it is, do it to others and it *will* be done to you. The best way to overcome the fear of what others are going to do to you is to generously contribute to others. If you contribute your time, wisdom, and material blessings, you will attract the same gifts to yourself.

Another factor in overcoming fear is to learn to listen to your conscience. Your conscience is an invisible governor built into the engine of your mind. This governor is installed to alert you when your engine is running too hot or when your unbridled instincts are starting to red line and approach overload.

When you reach for more than you deserve, self-justification creeps in. It is at this moment that your conscience alerts you to potential problems. It is extremely important that you don't override your conscience because when you do so, it always leads to trouble. If you are in the habit of overriding your conscience, it's a good idea to question your motives before taking an action. Ask yourself these simple questions:

- What is it about this situation that disturbs me?
- Why am I going against my better judgment and taking this action?
- What part does my ego play in my decision?

Your conscience is there to keep you out of trouble. When your conscience is clear, you have much less to worry about. This allows you to change your focus from thoughts of past misdeeds—which evoke fear of retribution or feelings of guilt—to more creative and empowering solutions.

Fear of Failure

One of the questions you asked yourself as part of the Full Recovery Action Plan exercise at the end of the last chapter was this: What are you afraid of? Now that you know the answer, what are you willing to do about it? You also answered the question: What would you attempt if you knew you couldn't fail? Are you aware that failure is self-defined and that nothing is a failure until you accept it as such? An easy way to manage fear is to change your focus and start asking yourself better questions. Examples of questions to ask yourself might be

- How can I use this experience to my advantage?
- Who can I help as a result of this experience?

- Who is already getting the results I want?
- Who knows how to overcome this fear?

These types of questions take the focus off the problem and point it toward a solution.

Also, try not to label your actions as a failure or a success. When you consider yourself as having failed, you subconsciously associate the experience with pain. When you associate an action with pain, you avoid it.

This makes it very easy to get frustrated or depressed whenever you attempt to learn something outside your comfort zone. When you feel frustrated and depressed, you typically don't perform at your best. Not performing at your best makes you feel more frustrated and depressed, and it leads to an endless cycle of nonperformance.

Instead, try looking at new situations like a scientist does when performing an experiment. You are just getting a result. Sometimes you get the results you want; other times you get something different from what you expected. Either way, you learned something. If you learned something, how can the experience be considered a failure? Just the fact that you learned what doesn't work makes the experience a success. Embracing this outlook is much easier on you than feeling like you've failed. It will also make you less likely to fear trying new things in the future.

If you learned something, how can the experience be considered a failure?

Another way to motivate yourself to try new things is to simply change your focus. Many fears are nothing more than misguided imaginings. Stop focusing on things you don't want, such as obstacles, fears, or old ways of looking at life, and start focusing on what you do want to have happen in your life. Don't look for the problem in the solution. Instead, rehearse your success in advance.

Your mind is set up to avoid pain and move toward happiness. The key is to train yourself to see every step in the direction of your goals as pleasurable, and every instance of fearful or lazy behavior as painful. You cannot fail; you can only get a result. The end result is ultimately a step toward reaching your goals. That alone can be considered a success.

To experience full recovery, you must develop a healthy relationship with fear. Fear is often found hiding behind the masks of anger, procrastination, resentment, inferiority, greed, and doubt.

I've heard these definitions for the acronym FEAR:

False Evidence Appears Real

Forget Everything and Run

Face Everything and Recover

I like the last one best because your ability to face your fears will directly influence not only your ability to recover from addiction but also your ability to reach your full potential.

Start focusing on what you want, and stop focusing on the perceived bad things that have happened to you. The question I put to you in the next chapter is, "How do you know that what you perceive as bad *is* really bad?"

Let's Review

- The miracle of recovery can be taught, learned, and duplicated.
- Living in fear is habit-forming.
- Fear keeps you from experiencing your full potential.
- Nothing has any meaning but the meaning you give it.
- You have a choice about how you talk to yourself.
- Changing your physiology outside changes the way you feel inside.
- No one can make you feel inadequate or rejected without your acceptance.
- Controlling your focus changes your state of mind.
- A working spirituality can overcome any fear.
- Living with a clear conscience keeps you focused on solutions instead of problems.
- Avoid labels like "success" and "failure." You are just getting a result.

FULL RECOVERY ACTION PLAN EXERCISES

At this time, I would like you to take out your Full Recovery Action Plan. You are going to create a new habit. A habit of "living in the solution," and it will add immense value to your life.

1. Write down five new affirmations that embody the new successful ideals that will now govern your life. Your affirmations should clearly spell out exactly the person you will become. Keep them brief and to the point. It is also a good idea to write each of them on a separate index

card or keep them on your computer where you can see them and read them aloud several times a day. Whenever you feel fear or doubt entering your consciousness, read your affirmations. Over time, your new empowering affirmations will become part of your subconscious.

2. Write down three separate instances when you felt completely empowered. These times should include your greatest moments and achievements. Make them emotional. Feel the joy of succeeding.

   This is a way of rehearsing success. Although you do not want to live in the past, this technique can be used to interrupt a negative thinking pattern. Whenever you find yourself focusing on a fearful situation or feel yourself slipping into doubt, consciously substitute your empowering successful thoughts in place of your fearful doubting thoughts. Really feel them.

   Change your physiology. Something as simple as standing tall, smiling, and moving with purpose can instantly change the way you feel. This is an easy way of developing a new positive habit.

3. Choose one thing you fear and answer the following questions about that fear:

   What are the negative consequences of NOT overcoming this fear?

   Who already knows how to overcome this fear?

   Can I use their experience to overcome my fear?

   How can I use my fearful experience to my advantage?

Whom can I help as a result of this experience?

What will be my reward when I conquer this fear?

When you wake each morning, ask God or your higher power for strength and guidance. Each night be thankful for the help you received to overcome limitation. Take this step of faith, even if you don't believe in God, and be ready to receive abundantly.

Perceptions

The difference between a flower and a weed is judgment.
—UNKNOWN

YOU'LL RECALL that at the end of the last chapter, I left you with a question: How do you know that what you perceive as bad is really bad? I have found that with every problem or challenge there is a lesson or opportunity to be gained. By challenging your habitual ways of thinking and your preconceived ideas, you will find empowering solutions to what used to be considered unsolvable problems.

Have you ever heard of Spencer Silver? If you are like most people, the answer is no. Back in the 1970s, he was a research scientist for the 3M Company. Silver spent much of his time and energy trying to develop a new super-strong adhesive. What did he accomplish? Well, not exactly what he was looking for. Silver ended up inventing glue that barely stuck to anything.

I'm sure he was disappointed, but rather than get depressed, Silver decided to ask himself a better question: "What can I do with this weak glue?" He talked to his peers and coworkers, but no one had any idea what to do with the stuff. Rather than get frustrated and just discard the product, Silver decided to continue on with his regular experiments and save the weak adhesive until the proper use for the product became apparent.

Fast-forward four years. Arthur Fry, a fellow scientist and associate of Silver's at 3M, happened to sing in a church choir. Fry was in the habit of using bookmarkers to keep his place in the hymnal. When the bookmarkers fell out and he'd lose his place, he was annoyed. After one such incident, Fry recalled Silver's adhesive and decided to coat his bookmarkers with it. After Fry applied the weak glue, he observed that although the markers would stay in place, he could easily lift them off again without damaging the pages in his book. Fry immediately began to brainstorm with Silver and others at 3M about the possible uses for this non-sticky glue. Out of Silver's adhesive mishap, the Post-it Note was born. Out of what most people would perceive as a problem, glue that didn't work, grew a multimillion-dollar product.

This is an excellent example of turning a perceived bad situation into a success.

Unless you live in a cave, you have no doubt heard of Michael Phelps and his outstanding achievement of winning eight gold medals at the 2008 Summer Olympics.

You might not be as familiar with Cullen Jones, who was also an Olympic gold medalist in swimming. He was part of the 4x100-meter freestyle relay team that helped Michael Phelps earn his Olympic gold medal record.

Cullen is an African-American, born in the Bronx in New York City—one of toughest inner-city neighborhoods in America. It is certainly not known as an area that produces world-class swimmers.

As a young boy Cullen had the misfortune of almost drowning in a public pool. He was dragged from the pool unconscious and luckily was revived through CPR.

Rather than having their son live in fear of and stay away from the water, Cullen's parents decided to enroll him in swimming lessons. Out of this unfortunate incident came one of the world's greatest swimmers. This is another example of taking a potential negative, or what could be perceived of as a bad situation, and turning it into a positive.

The next time you are tempted to cower in the face of disappointment or adversity, try looking for the lesson. Sometimes you will be able to realize the lesson by asking yourself the proper questions. In other instances, you'll need the benefit of time to uncover the lesson.

I would like to share some of my own expertise in this area. In the introduction, I mentioned that "luckily" my higher power intervened in my life and I was involved in a horrible accident. That unfortunate event turned out to be a blessing in disguise. But believe me, when that accident occurred, I considered it anything but lucky.

My perception of a good life at that time was owning the world's nicest Harley, possessing an unending supply of booze, pot, and coke, and having the free time to overindulge in all of the above—uninterrupted.

As I descended deeper into the insanity of addiction, my decisions became increasingly irrational. My wife lived in constant fear of what I would do next. She tried pleading, arguing, reasoning with me, but I would hear none of it. Eventually, I had to make a decision. Would I choose my family and recovery or my addiction?

I can't find the words to accurately describe the sense of self-loathing and isolation I was feeling during this difficult time. Somewhere deep inside me must have still lingered a spark of the divine spirit, but in my constant state of intoxication, I was unable to draw it out. The disease of addiction is one of selfishness and self-justification, and I had been fine-tuning my talents in both areas.

I remember more than once telling my wife that she and everything else would go before I would stop parking my Harley in the house or even consider giving up drinking and drugging. I told her, "You knew what I was when you married me." That was another delusion, because as you are probably aware, addiction is a progressive, terminal disease that always gets worse over time.

I finally convinced myself that my overbearing wife was the reason for my unhappiness. If I could just get away from her and the pressure she put on me to change my behavior, I wouldn't have to drink and drug so much. Addiction had won. I was leaving my responsibilities out west and heading east.

On the day before I was to abandon my family because, of course, it was their fault I was out of control, I had a horrific motorcycle accident. I was done for. I was unconscious, in the desert, forty miles from anything that even resembled civilization. Miraculously, someone found me down in a ditch off the side of the road and called the state troopers. To this day I have no idea who made that call. A helicopter showed up and transported me to the hospital.

I was drunk, in shock, and insane. I had a broken back, multiple compound fractures of the fibula and tibia in my right leg, and severe head trauma that required hundreds of stitches, along with several other broken bones and injuries. I was told I would probably lose my leg. Now this could be perceived as a bad situation, wouldn't you agree?

Amid all the chaos, my wife—you know, the one who was holding me back?—showed up, which was a miracle in and of itself. She met with doctors, talked to insurance representatives, and made sure I was receiving the best care possible. Rather than operating on my leg, the hospital staff spent a few days getting me stabilized in preparation for transferring me to another hospital. I was put in traction, and the pain was absolutely incredible. They eventually transferred me to a new hospital where a doctor, fresh out of medical school, performed a very radical procedure for that time. He implanted nineteen screws and other hardware, crafted a titanium plate for a shinbone, and ended up saving my leg.

Due to my addictions, as well as the overwhelming physical pain, I was unable to muster much gratitude. My diagnosis for the foreseeable future was pain, suffering, and a bad limp. I was used to fighting and I was in the fight of my life. The more they told me I would not walk properly, the more defiant I became. I realize now that God gave me even my anger and character defects for a good reason. I refused to lie down. I *would* walk normally.

I could easily view the accident and subsequent rehabilitation as a negative memory. Instead, I choose to look at this situation, from start to finish, as the biggest blessing of my life. You might wonder how this could possibly be a blessing, so let me explain.

During that time of my life I considered myself an atheist, or at best an agnostic. I lived in a drunken world of my own making where I played the God role. I believed I was dangerous, so I was. My intoxicated existence was savage.

When I was told my leg would probably be amputated, it was

a reality check. I remember thinking, "I don't know if you are out there, God, but if you are, I can really use a hand right now."

That act, in and of itself, was the beginning of my journey back to sanity. Just the willingness to believe that God could and would help me, if I asked, was the humblest of starting points.

I look back on all the so-called coincidences that happened and I know God's loving hand was guiding me home. The stranger who found me in the desert . . . the young doctor whose "experimental operation" saved my leg . . . the wife I was leaving making sure I was receiving the best possible treatment . . . the rehabilitation ending more successfully than anyone would have thought. I truly believe that these stars did not align by chance.

I would like to tell you that this horrendous experience is what convinced me to get sober, but such is not the case. During my hospital stay, I had people smuggle in booze. When I was released from the hospital, I was living in a second-floor apartment. I would throw my crutches over the balcony railing, hop down the stairs on my backside, and then grab the crutches and walk more than a mile to the closest bar. I even fabricated a beer holder for each crutch so I could drink on the long hop back to my apartment. All this was done while I was still wearing a back brace. Addiction wielded that much power over me.

Looking back, I knew then that I had a drinking problem, but my perception was that I could control it. In my delusional thinking, I convinced myself that this latest accident was just an unfortunate incident that could have happened to anyone. I didn't even consider trying to get sober. I did not understand the progressive, terminal nature of my disease, which was about to kick into overdrive. I was racing toward new bottoms. There would be many more accidents, financial ruin, and near insanity looming on the horizon.

Although it took six more years of suffering and insanity for me to even attempt to get sober, that moment when I cried out to my Maker is the taproot from which a new life has blossomed. Years later, when I had finally reached bottom, that moment in the hospital flashed into my consciousness like a beacon of hope, and once again, I asked God for help.

Had I not had that accident, I might have left my wife and my son and never looked back. Instead, to this day I am still with my wife. We have been married for thirty-seven years as of this writing and enjoy the most beautiful and purest relationship two people can share. The love we have for each other is precious and priceless. She is my soul mate and a gift from God.

My son is the expression of my love and joy. He has grown into an outstanding young man. He is honest, compassionate, industrious, and honorable. I enjoy his humor and companionship more than words can describe.

We have lived as a loving, supportive family, and the Creator has truly smiled on us.

So, as you can see, some of the worst things that have ever happened to you can turn out to be the best if you're willing to give it time, look for the lessons, and challenge your perceptions.

Every setback carries with it a greater seed of opportunity. To locate the seeds of opportunity, take these steps and the lessons will be revealed:

1. Look for and acknowledge any mistakes that were made.
2. After acknowledging them, don't waste time reliving them over and over in your mind. This is just mentally repeating your mistakes and often leads to depression, guilt, shame, and inevitably more mistakes.
3. Recognize the positive impacts or lessons to be learned from this perceived setback.
4. Instead of mentally rehearsing your mistakes, take a different action based on what you have learned.
5. Study the results you are getting.
6. Keep changing your actions until you achieve the results you are seeking.

As we change our perceptions and come to a full understanding of our past and our present, we can begin to move forward with confidence. The ability to change how you perceive things is closely tied to your willingness to examine your beliefs. Beliefs are the steering mechanism for this journey known as life. Your beliefs are merely mental acceptance of a particular reality based on your past experiences. Your beliefs came into existence as a result of the trust or confidence you placed in some individual,

Your beliefs are merely mental acceptance of a particular reality based on your past experiences. Your beliefs came into existence as a result of the trust or confidence you placed in some individual, group, or thing.

group, or thing. Your beliefs became habitual through acceptance and repetition.

To be able to stop drinking and drugging, I needed to change my beliefs. But as I began to work toward full recovery, I began to question my beliefs once again. To be truly sober, and not just abstinent, I had to change my belief from one of self-reliance to reliance on God. The question I have for you is: How do you know that your habitual beliefs don't need upgrading? As I stated earlier, fear often keeps you from questioning your beliefs. Fear is a bogeyman you must be willing to push past if you are to achieve a life of abundance.

To be truly sober, and not just abstinent, I had to change my belief from one of self-reliance to reliance on God.

Let's examine some of your core beliefs regarding career, wealth, relationships, religion, and God.

You've heard me say, "Ask better questions and you'll receive better answers." Intelligent questions focus your creative energy on empowering solutions. What types of thoughts or questions are directing your life? Let's face it: A belief is really just the answer to a question. Your mind is constantly weighing options. It's always evaluating the pros and cons of a situation by posing "what-if" questions. What will happen if I take a particular action? From simple actions, such as what clothing to wear or what route to drive to work, to more complex actions, such as whether divorce is your only option, your thoughts and questions are entangled and influential.

How do you start your day? Do you open your eyes in the morning and start asking questions like these: Why do I have to wake up? Why do I have to go to work? How am I going to make it through the day? After showering and having breakfast, do you continue with: How come I can't afford a nicer car? Who thought So-and-So would make a good boss? How come I can't make enough money to pay the bills? And so on.

Did you recognize yourself in some of those early-morning questions? Unfortunately, many people do and repeat the same process—every day. Such thoughts are based in the belief that you do not have the power of choice or that you lack the ability to get what you want out of life. If you start your day with these thoughts, based in those negative beliefs, it's very difficult to feel motivated, never mind inspired or empowered.

These types of questions or beliefs are based in fear and doubt. They instantly give your mind a negative reference. This negative reference starts all kinds of chemical reactions in your brain. These reactions alert your nervous system and put unneeded stress on your body. This stress causes pain and depression, which invites more fear-based, weak-minded questions.

These negative beliefs don't inspire abundance. Instead, they create depression. These questions assume a lack of control or direction on the part of the person doing the asking. Remember, whether you learned this habit or developed it through laziness, you have a choice. You can change your thoughts and beliefs. You also have the choice of surrendering your freedom to choose to someone else. An excess of people are out there who would be more than happy to make decisions for you. Just as destructive habits and beliefs are formed through repetition, positive habits and beliefs can be created through choice, discipline, and repetition.

Are you struggling in an unfulfilling career because you do not believe you can do better? Are you willing to let your boss decide how much you are worth? Wouldn't you rather invest your time creating a career path that you can believe in? If you want more, it's time to contribute more.

Developing more empowering beliefs is a process. Start by asking yourself better questions. Here are some examples:

- How am I going to create an exciting future for myself today?
- Who can I attract to myself that will assist me in this endeavor?
- How can I be a positive influence on my community?
- What service can I render that will assure my success?
- How can I offer better-quality goods and services to my employer or my customers?
- Whose load can I lighten today with my compassion?
- Where do I want to invest my valuable time and energy to achieve a maximum return?

Start changing your old beliefs by asking yourself these types of questions, keeping in mind what you have already learned about changing your physiology. Hold your head high, breathe deeply, throw your shoulders back, and feel what it's like to be powerful and in charge of your life. These questions, answered and practiced daily, can start your day in a constructive way.

It's usually about this time that the old beliefs start playing in your head. You know the ones . . . the negative, defeatist beliefs that fight for survival by reminding you of past failures. These are the nagging fears and doubts that keep you from realizing your true potential. These beliefs are nothing more than bad habits.

Remember, you have been afforded the power of choice. You can choose to hang on to your old unworkable beliefs and habits, or you can decide to change. Even your most deeply rooted beliefs are subject to change, or at least reinterpretation, when you are properly motivated.

To illustrate my point, I would like you to go back in time to when you were a small child. What were your beliefs about your parents? Was your father the strongest, most powerful man you knew? Was your mother loving and all-knowing? Maybe your mother was the strongest, most powerful person you knew?

It doesn't really matter. The point is that when you think about it, as you matured your opinions about your parents changed. You began to see them as adults with some good and some not-so-good qualities. Maybe your mother and father got a divorce and feelings have been damaged. Or perhaps you have even more admiration and respect for your parents after witnessing them meet challenging situations with love and commitment. Either way, I think you'll agree that over time, as you matured and your understanding changed, so did your beliefs about your parents.

This exercise can be done with any subject. Maybe when you were young you wanted to be president or a movie star. But as you got older those careers didn't hold the same allure. Perhaps you don't want the media prying into your personal life, or maybe you just don't like public speaking, in which case both careers would not be comfortable. The point is that when properly motivated, you changed your beliefs.

Your Beliefs About Career

Are you happy with your present career? Do you believe that you are on the best possible career path? If not, it's probably because you are not fulfilling your destiny. Your destiny and desires, as far as a career is concerned, should involve doing something you enjoy. You were not created to live a dull, uninspired existence. When you enjoy doing something, you typically do it well, and it doesn't feel like work.

Years ago, I heard this story about Kenny Rogers. He was being questioned about all the successes he had achieved in the music business. The interviewer made a statement to the effect that Rogers's parents probably tried to talk him out of being a singer and must have been surprised by his achievements.

Rogers responded that the opposite was true. He said that when he was a young man, he was discussing career choices with his mother. Like most people, Rogers did not know what he wanted to be when he grew up. His mother asked him what he liked to do. He responded that he liked to entertain folks by singing and playing the guitar. His mother told him that's what he should do for a job. She went on to say that if he enjoyed entertaining folks and made that his career, he'd never have to work a day in his life. How's that for good advice!

The interesting part is that when we do what we like, we do it with enthusiasm and we usually do it well. We bring a passion and energy to the task that separates us from the person merely performing a task for a paycheck. Enthusiastic energy is contagious.

What do you enjoy doing? How can you work your God-given desires and talents into your career? This process of discovery is grounded in truth. That's why you started your Full Recovery Action Plan by discovering your strengths, weaknesses, and beliefs about yourself. That step is the basis of character building. Character always precedes long-term prosperity.

We all need to earn a living. Most people work eight hours per day, which leaves eight hours for sleep and eight hours of free time. Start today by making that free time actually work for you. Turn off the TV and start applying yourself. Time is one denomination in which we are all equal. Rich or poor, black or white, man or woman, we all get the same twenty-four hours in a day. How we choose to invest that time will decide, to a great extent, whether we live an abundant lifestyle or a poor one. It certainly applies to material wealth, but it also applies to physical, spiritual, emotional, and educational wealth.

How do you invest your free time? What do you consider success? What are your desired outcomes? These are important questions to consider.

Success and abundance to a missionary are not the same as success and abundance to an investment banker. You are the only one who can decide if you are succeeding or not.

I have heard recovering alcoholics describe a successful day as any day they stay sober. I have also met multimillionaires who have confided in me that they felt unsuccessful because they were worth only $10 million, and by their definition, to be a success you needed to be worth $50 million.

Feeling successful depends on the self-imposed rules you set up. That's right. You decide if you are successful or not. You are a success if you believe you are.

As long as I take action toward achieving my goals, I consider myself a success. This makes it much easier for me to feel positive about myself, which encourages me to take even more action.

Your Beliefs About Wealth

Directly related to your beliefs about career and success are your beliefs about wealth. What do you believe about money or material prosperity? Is money good? Is it the root of all evil? In an earlier exercise you filled in the blank in the statement "Money is ______________________." What was your answer? Most people I've interviewed say they want more money, yet the most common view people have of money ends up being that it's "the root of all evil."

Can you see how having such a negative association with money makes it very difficult to stay motivated when working to attain it? Where did your concept of money or prosperity originate? Is your present belief regarding money serving you well? If you are lacking in money or prosperity the answer probably is no.

Many people speak of money as being evil or corrupting. But they misquote the Bible when they say, "Money is the root of all evil." What the Bible actually says is, "For the love of money is the root of all evil, which while some coveted after, they have erred from faith, and pierced themselves through with many sorrows."

I think that verse is talking about greed, which could be described as the love of money to the extreme. It is an unhealthy habit that no person of good character would endorse. When we corrupt our morals to obtain money, we do ourselves and the world a disservice. But make no mistake about it: money is a valuable tool in our modern society. Money provides food, clothing, housing, education, and health care for you and your loved ones. It pays for science and art projects to benefit mankind.

Money does not guarantee happiness, but it is much easier to be happy with an abundance of money than to live in poverty. We've all seen pictures of Third World countries where starvation and disease are a way of life. It is very difficult to be happy under those circumstances. Having an abundance of money allows you the opportunity to help those less fortunate than yourself. In that respect, it is surely good.

- How much money do you want? You need to come up with an exact amount to have any chance of getting it.
- What are you willing to give for it? There is no such thing as something for nothing. Everything has its price.
- Whom do you want to share it with? Remember the mirror. If you want more money, contribute more to the happiness and success of others. Giving and receiving are two sides of the same coin.
- How can your ability to demonstrate prosperity inspire others in your community?

These types of thoughts and questions, when answered intelligently, lead to more empowering beliefs than the well-worn "money is the root of all evil" we have all been sold.

I once had a friend tell me that money is just "God in circulation," hence the words "In God We Trust" printed on American currency. I don't know if I would go that far, but viewing money from this frame of reference is much more inspiring and healthy than simply accepting financial scarcity.

Money is not bad or evil. Money is a tool to be used and a commodity to be exchanged. Nothing replaces money in the situations in which money is required. For example, you can't pay the mortgage with love; the bank prefers cash.

Your Beliefs About Relationships

What are you seeking in a relationship? Do you want a spouse or a partner? Do you believe it's possible to enjoy a monogamous long-term marriage or relationship? Are you fearless enough to expose yourself to potential heartbreak? Or are you all get and no give, taking what's easy and moving on when the going gets tough? Don't be too quick to give up on your current relationship. I hear it all the time: we are so different, or we have grown apart. In many cases this is a cop-out. There is a reason you are different. You were made that way. Try complementing each other by appreciating one another for who you are. Your shortcomings might be your partner's strength. Try focusing on what you like about your spouse or partner and stop focusing on what you don't like. Changing your focus changes your reality.

Love is our greatest need. True love is not selfish. Love gives rather than takes. Love learns to forget. If you insist on keeping a scorecard, you will never be able to develop your relationship at the deepest levels. When you forgive, it encourages others to do the same. Your spouse and family should be cherished as one of your greatest blessings and not taken for granted. When you are old or sick, your money can't come visit you.

In many cases, a perceived need for money interferes with our need for love and sex with our spouse. Money and financial disagreements are high on the list of reasons for the ballooning divorce rate in the United States. Ego, selfishness, and stubbornness play a pivotal role in this cycle. Rather than focusing on the qualities that caused the couple to fall in love to begin with (sense of humor, caring, and honesty), money becomes the all-consuming basis for the relationship.

Self-justified actions take place when partners don't get what they think they need. These inappropriate actions often grow into resentment. Feelings that they are giving too much begin to ferment. These selfish attitudes provide ample fodder for senseless arguments that bring disharmony into the home. Love, children, camaraderie, and passion are pushed aside for the cheap and easily replaceable commodity known as money. This relatively new cycle of selfishness and stubbornness ultimately breaks the family apart. Unfortunately, the participants, their children, and society as a whole are losers.

Try to recall something you were upset about two weeks, two months, or two years ago. If you're like most people I've interviewed, you will not be able to come up with an answer. If these situations are so trivial that you can't even remember them, then they certainly aren't worth ruining your day or upsetting the relationship with your loved ones. It's ego plain and simple that demands to be right.

The next time you are about to put your ego or financial needs ahead of your spouse's needs, stop and ask yourself this question: Do I want to be right or do I want to be happy? I'll choose happy. Another question might be, how important is it?

Your Beliefs About Religion and God

Now let's focus on your beliefs in regard to religion and God. Do you remember what you were taught as a small child? Was God a kind and loving figure or an authoritative one who only punished people? Was God fickle, only loving you as long as you obeyed, and damning you for eternity if you didn't? Was God represented as a he or a she? Maybe you were taught that there is no God, only Mother Nature. If you disobeyed God's rules, what were the consequences? Were you forgiven or would you burn in hell?

The twenty-first century has witnessed a mass exodus from organized religion. I believe this was caused in part by the tendency of many religions to place strict obedience to traditions ahead of spirituality. Spiritual development hinges on the ability to question, grow, and change as our understanding dictates.

Organized religion tries desperately to force the same dogma on an adult as it does a five-year-old. Often, if you question or seek guidance outside the teachings of the church, you are reprimanded and possibly considered a sinner. In some less tolerant sects, you might even be excommunicated, guaranteeing you a trip to hell. For most people, just being shunned by their peers or their congregation is deterrent enough to keep them from questioning the church's doctrines. For others, the idea of eternal damnation for these types of temporary transgressions is not worth the gamble. It's easier to go through the motions than risk the worst.

Taking the first steps toward achieving sobriety requires a certain level of belief. But are you willing to go further? Are you able to push beyond your self-imposed limitations and believe in the true source of power, which for lack of a better term we call God? Are you ready to challenge your belief in what's possible and develop the same quality of faith that allowed you to get sober to begin with? It comes down to a matter of choice. In order to develop that belief, you have to ask the right questions.

If you have chosen recovery, you have begun to take personal responsibility for your spiritual beliefs. You have begun to move beyond the beliefs of others and to build your own belief system. Too often, though, we stop too soon in this process; we hesitate to develop beliefs that will enable us to move beyond sobriety to realize full recovery.

Once again, fear keeps us from experiencing all the joy and abundance that a spiritually guided personal relationship with the Creator will bring us. One easy way to overcome fear is to believe that God has individualized himself in you through your soul. You would not be here participating in this reality if God did not will it.

Think about it. You came from somewhere. You experience this life. Then you go somewhere else. You appeared. You are here. Then you disappear.

At a gut level, most people have some sort of belief in a Creative Intelligence or Supreme Being, however misguided it might be. Call it nature. Call it a higher power. Call it God—or anything else you want. But like it or not, there is an order and a rhythm to the universe. Have you ever thought about the word *universe*? When you break it down—uni-verse—it means "one-song." You are part of that universe. You are a note in that song. Align yourself with the Creator's purpose for you in this world. Do your best to carry it out and you will know peace. We all have a purpose. God is cause. We are effect. Maybe you have been playing the wrong note in this symphony we call life.

For years, I was living a godless life. It was self-interest run riot, and of course, it produced godless results. Addiction lowered my consciousness, blurred the vision in my mind's eye, and poisoned my soul. I deluded myself into believing I was independent and a rebel. Modern society hates dependency of any sort, even dependency on God. The result of all this misuse of my willpower was my dependence on drugs and alcohol.

I am not alone. Many times, as people mature, they try living with the God of their youth and somehow don't feel fulfilled or even connected. They start confusing religion and spirituality, even though the two are completely separate. Religion is a man-made set of rules, while spirituality is a birthright, a belief that connects us to the universal consciousness we call God. This confusion often creates a sense of separation, leading to the worship of independence and individuality.

A life of self-interest and materialism, void of any spiritual connection, is a lonely, unfulfilled life. It's a horrible awakening to realize that you have traded spiritual apathy, a form of living that doesn't work, for materialism that doesn't work either.

The emptiness of the "God-hole" grows and the ego tries to fill the vacuum. A good way to look at the word *ego* is to view it as an acronym that stands for "Easing God Out." We ease God out and attempt to take over the duties. The ego tries filling the void with food, drugs, alcohol, money, sex, power, bravado, and many other temporary distractions. None of which brings true happiness and peace of mind. The only way to fill the God-hole is with God.

That means asking better questions about yourself and your place in the cosmos. It takes prayer and meditation, as well as the willingness to change.

Prayer is speaking to God and meditation is simply listening for the answer. Both are necessary to develop the moral compass and fearless nature needed to lead a life of true wealth and prosperity. How many people have succeeded in amassing great monetary wealth or personal fame or have even achieved a level of sobriety, yet still end up living in fear and disharmony with their fellow human beings?

To be truly wealthy you must possess peace of mind, which can only be accomplished by living a moral and ethical lifestyle. A lifestyle led by a "God-consciousness" and a commitment to your fellow men and women.

To be truly wealthy you must possess peace of mind, which can only be accomplished by living a moral and ethical lifestyle led by a "God-consciousness" and a commitment to your fellow men and women.

The first words of the Lord's Prayer sum it up: "Our Father." We are all in this together—brothers and sisters under one Creator. The word *individual,* so exalted in our society, has actually been perverted from its original meaning, which is "part of the whole, not separate from the whole."

Sure, we all have our own ideas and want to be appreciated for who we are . . . and in reality, this is how it should be. We run into problems when we insist on being the "all" instead of part of the whole. The truth is that we all need each other to succeed. No one knows everything.

Part of the Whole

If you really believe you can stand alone, or that you are truly self-made, try this exercise.

Look around the space you are currently occupying and ponder these questions (for this exercise, I'm assuming it is a room inside a building):

- Do you know how to make the paint on the walls or the carpet on the floor? Do you even know the process or chemical composition of either?
- Where did the lumber, steel, and plastic come from to build the furniture? Do you have the skill needed to manufacture it?
- Do you have the ability to grow, package, or transport the food in this room to yourself or others?
- Where did the electricity or the gas used for the lights and the heating and cooling come from?

Do you get the idea?

And if you doubt the existence of a higher power, ask yourself if you

- Can create any of the elements or raw materials needed to manufacture anything at all?
- Can you create atoms with their protons and electrons swirling in perfect harmony or, at the quantum level, the quarks and bosons that make up the subatomic world in which we live?

If you're honest with yourself, you'll acknowledge that we are all in this together, and we all need to help each other. Contribution by all assures the continually expanding quality of life we all enjoy.

The best way we can demonstrate our belief in God is to demonstrate our willingness to help one another. Without this willingness, we can never achieve full recovery. Remember this: You can quicken your journey to happiness and success by focusing your talents and abilities on helping others achieve a better life.

Your perceptions and beliefs regarding your career, your idea of wealth, your relationships, and your concept of religion and God are meant to be continuously evolving. Trying to remain rigid or static will only result in frustration and disappointment. You are now ready to answer the tough questions and examine your core beliefs. Open-mindedness and willingness will help you to move beyond limitation and guide you to truth. These points will be reinforced throughout the entire book. So don't be surprised. Those who forget are doomed to repeat.

Let's Review

- Challenge your perception of good and bad, right and wrong.
- Some of your perceived failures can, upon examination, be your biggest blessings.
- Beliefs are a mental acceptance of a particular reality.
- Beliefs become habitual through repetition.
- Thoughts and questions are connected and often one and the same.
- Choose today to start developing and asking yourself better questions.
- What you focus your thoughts on inevitably manifests itself in your life.
- You can make a decision right now to abandon limiting beliefs in favor of ones that serve you better.
- Fear often hinders you from questioning your beliefs.

FULL RECOVERY ACTION PLAN EXERCISES

Now it's time to take out your Full Recovery Action Plan.

1. Take a moment to write down the details about one situation you perceive as bad, and then try to find the seed of opportunity in it. It might be the loss of a job or of a relationship that could lead you to a new career or a new relationship. You may be currently experiencing some sort of challenge in your finances or with your health. The seed of opportunity might be as simple as learning a lesson or figuring out what hasn't worked in the past.

These types of distinctions are very valuable and should be accepted so they are not repeated.

2. What types of thoughts or questions do you ask yourself at the start of each day? If you don't remember, when you wake up tomorrow, write them down.
3. What types of questions do you need to ask yourself to start your day in an inspired way? Write down four questions.
4. If you are in a relationship, what do you enjoy about your partner?
5. What would you change about your partner and why?
6. What changes can you make in yourself to make the relationship better?
7. What are the reasons you continue in your present career?
8. If you could choose a new career what would it be and why?
9. Do you have as much money as you want?
10. Do your beliefs about money produce results? What are those results?
11. Who do you consider successful, and why?
12. What new rules can you develop that will help you feel successful today?
13. How can you help others to become successful?

14. What are you looking for in a spiritual connection?
15. Are you happy with your current beliefs about God? If not, are you willing to change them?
16. What do you believe is the Creator's purpose for you?

The following list of questions shows examples of the types of questions I ask myself each morning. Commit the following questions to memory to help you develop a new habit of asking better questions that will strengthen your beliefs. Whenever your old negative belief systems start playing in your head, consciously substitute all or part of this list to change your focus. Asking these types of questions can help you start your day in a constructive way. Better questions produce better answers. Better answers ensure better results.

- How am I going to create an exciting future for myself today?
- Who can I attract to myself that will assist me in this endeavor?
- How can I be a positive influence on my community?
- What service can I render that will assure my success?
- How can I offer better-quality goods and services to my employer or my customers?
- Whose load can I lighten today with my compassion?
- Where do I want to invest my valuable time and energy to achieve a maximum return?

The Gift of Discomfort

All experience hath shewn, that mankind are more disposed to suffer, while evils are sufferable, than to right themselves by abolishing the forms to which they are accustomed.
—THE DECLARATION OF INDEPENDENCE

THE FOUNDING FATHERS of the United States of America spelled it out clearly: human beings will suffer almost anything before they are willing to change. This holds true even if we are aware that we are suffering and realize there's a solution to our suffering. Most people will try to ignore their problems, or change their focus to something else, rather than take the appropriate action to change. It is only when the pain and suffering are so overwhelming and no longer tolerable that action is finally taken. Like it or not, pain is the best friend of change. This is why it is so important to lower your threshold for pain.

Now, you might be thinking, It's bad enough that you are making me look at myself and question my lifelong beliefs. But now you're asking me to feel *more* pain. How can this possibly be good? Well, let me explain.

As we get older and mature, we develop an acute sensitivity to pain. It's not so much physical discomfort, like we experienced in childhood. It's more often emotional and mental pain. Psychologists have been studying this phenomenon for years. Sigmund Freud has been given much credit for originating the pain/pleasure principle in modern psychoanalysis. As far back as 300 BC, however, Aristotle realized the importance of this principle for humanity: "We may lay it down that pleasure is a movement, a movement by which the soul as a whole is consciously brought into its normal state of being; and that pain is the opposite."

Aristotle confirms in his rhetoric that the soul in its normal state is meant to be happy. I really like that affirmation. When our soul isn't happy, we can consciously move it in that direction. When confronted with pain, we can choose to take action and change back to our normal state, which is pleasure.

Most people in the Western Hemisphere live a fairly safe existence. Unlike during prehistoric times, we are no longer hunted as food. We enjoy comfortable shelter. We have a large military to protect us from foreign invasion. We inhabit nations with laws and adequate police protection. What our brains focus on now is saving us from emotional pain.

When the brain is faced with discomfort—learning a new skill, making a difficult decision, or failing in any number of situations, for example—it relates the experience to pain. It tries to shield us from the experience. The brain fears pain. This is evidenced by our approach-avoidance to learning new skills, as we get older.

Now you understand why most adults don't succeed at the level of their abilities, never mind reach their full potential. Can you see the importance of choosing intelligently what you associate with pain or pleasure?

Your brain is designed to help you avoid pain and seek out pleasure. A problem arises when you become aware that you are living below your capabilities, and this awareness becomes painful. You might ask, If people are not happy with their lives and find them painful, why don't they take action to change? The answer is they do take action. They self-medicate with alcohol, tobacco, food, drugs, sex, work, gambling, and many other distractions. These are just enough to keep the pain sufferable, as was noted in the Declaration of Independence. When self-medicating no longer works, we seek other options.

The reason for lowering your threshold to pain is to save time and empower you to instantly change your life. The quicker and more intensely you feel pain, the faster you will change. The quicker you change, the less pain you will ultimately have to endure. Why wait to hit the bottom when you can step off the elevator on any floor you choose?

Once you become aware that some of your beliefs and habits are no longer serving you well, try taking immediate action rather than deceiving yourself, ignoring the issue, or self-medicating. Why not try dealing with the issue immediately?

If you intelligently choose to make a change after weighing your options, the easiest way to stay the course is to associate massive amounts of discomfort and suffering with the habit or belief you want to change. The next step is to associate overwhelming joy and gratification with your new more empowering behavior.

You may think that sounds too easy. Or maybe you believe just the opposite—that it's impossible. Perhaps you think that you can't change the way you've always felt. The truth is, *it is that easy*. You do get to decide how to feel and what you want to believe. It's undeniably true that humans move away from

Associate massive amounts of discomfort and suffering with the habit or belief you want to change, then associate overwhelming joy and gratification with your new more empowering behavior.

perceived pain and toward perceived pleasure. You should note that I said "perceived pain" and "perceived pleasure." Once again, nothing has any meaning but the meaning you give it. Pain and happiness are in the mind of the perceiver.

Why wait until the pain and discomfort become unbearable to take action? It is much easier and less painful in the long run to deal with challenges immediately.

We who have decided through our own choices to live a higher existence of unlimited abundance have realized that by changing our beliefs and lowering our threshold for pain, we can empower ourselves instantly. We have declared our own independence!

This pain and pleasure scenario is constantly being used to influence your behavior. Most successful politicians and advertisers employ some form of "risk versus reward," "pain or pleasure," "winner or loser" psychology. Take insurance companies, for example. You probably have seen something like this on a TV commercial. During the setup of the ad, they show you a happy, loving family who are spending quality time together in their nice home.

The next scene has fire trucks arriving at the house, which is in flames. Of course, the children are frightened and huddled up against mom and dad. Then the advertiser flashes the name of the insurance company, and the camera pans out to show you an insurance agent already on the scene as the parents explain how they just lost everything.

The commercial continues with the insurance company giving the homeowners a check for their losses. The smiling family thanks the agent and tells him they don't know how they would have survived without their insurance company. Finally, they hit you with a catchy slogan: Don't you deserve peace of mind?

This is plain old hurt and happiness, pain and pleasure psychology. They hook your attention with fear and show you the pain. Then they sell you the happiness and peace of mind. Such advertising plays on your fears and emotions, but the underlying message is simple: Give us your money and we will take care of you. If you don't, you might get hurt.

Beer commercials do the same thing, just a little more subtly. They show you a beautiful sunlit beach with young, gorgeous people frolicking or playing volleyball (while drinking their product, of course). Then someone else arrives on the scene who obviously doesn't drink their brand of beer. This person is shunned or mocked—an emotionally painful experience. It's simple psychology. Drink our brand and you'll be cool. Don't, and you'll be a loser or an outcast. No one wants to be a loser or an outcast, so what do people do? If they can relate to the scenario, preferably at an emotional or subconscious level, they will follow the advertisers' directions and purchase the product being promoted. Strange as it is, most people don't even realize why they are taking the action they are taking. Ivan Pavlov called this a "conditioned response."

Most of us recall learning about this Russian scientist who observed in one of his experiments that every day at feeding time, the dogs would begin to salivate while waiting to be fed. He began to ring a bell just prior to giving the dogs food. After a few weeks, Pavlov discovered that even though no food was within sight or smell of the dogs, all he had to do was ring the bell and the dogs would begin to salivate. By repetition and stimulation, he was able to produce a predetermined result and alter the behavior of the dogs. Advertisers and politicians do the same thing to us, and the most effective way of getting us to take action is by using the pain and pleasure scenario.

This "pain and discomfort" versus "happiness and pleasure" dynamic is constantly at work in other areas of our lives too. For example, how does someone wind up in a rehab program or some twelve-step meeting? It's not because life is wonderful and one big party. On the contrary, for most people the party was over a long time ago.

They show up because they are in massive pain and out of ideas. They are in emotional and spiritual pain and are usually suffering financially and physically as well. It's said that to be willing to take the steps these programs require, most people must have "hit bottom." The interesting thing is that people have to decide for themselves how low they are willing to go.

Some people's bottom is actually very high. Maybe they don't like not being in control of their faculties, or perhaps they had a few minor mishaps that they considered embarrassing. Others have run the gamut from divorce and DWI to jails and mental institutions before they decide that they have had enough. The one thing these two groups have in common, though, is that they both decided they had experienced enough pain. Ultimately, it's pain that caused them to take certain actions to change. If they stay in recovery long enough, life gets better and more pleasurable.

The terrific physical beating I placed on myself was not enough to convince me that I needed to get sober. What finally pushed me to seek out other solutions was the emotional trauma and spiritual bankruptcy that accompanied active addiction. I had to get to the point of wanting to die before I looked for other options. Pain is the common denominator among all people who enter recovery.

With this new understanding of how your mind reacts to pain and pleasure, it's interesting to dissect some of your past actions. When we are faced with two options that seem painful, we always choose the one we perceive to be the lesser of the pains.

A perfect example of this is repeated, year after year, at every college in the country, and you might even have participated. I'll set the scene. It's one month before final exams. Do you start studying immediately, or do you wait until the night before exams to start studying? Maybe you start sometime in between.

If you start right away, you might be the type of person who associates negative or painful feelings with not being prepared and positive, pleasurable feelings with getting an "A" on the test. Perhaps you just want to keep your workload manageable or to get the task out of the way, so for the next four weeks you won't have to worry about not being prepared.

If you wait until the last week to start studying, you might be the type of person who associates negative feelings or pain with wasting time studying when you could be out with your friends or watching TV. You may also associate positive feelings with partying or being lazy.

What if you start cramming on the night before exams? Then it's likely that when you were faced with two potential negatives (studying all night and trying to pass, or not studying and failing the exam), you concluded it was less painful to stay up all night cramming, with the hope that you would pass, than it was to not study at all and fail your exam. In addition to the pain, you might also associate pleasure with passing the exam so you could stay in school and continue the party.

This is how the brain works. It is constantly evaluating pain and pleasure. When faced with two pains, it chooses the lesser of the two.

This is true even regarding something as unfortunate and insane as suicide. The person committing the act becomes convinced that it is less painful to destroy him- or herself than to continue living a tortured existence.

What's interesting is that we all decide what we consider uncomfortable or painful versus pleasurable. We also decide how much suffering and unpleasantness we are willing to endure before changing our unworkable habits. A habit is just a behavior pattern that is acquired through repetition. Many habits become automatic and nearly involuntary. If you have ever tried to quit smoking, drinking, or overeating, you know what I mean.

We all decide what we consider uncomfortable or painful versus pleasurable. We also decide how much suffering and unpleasantness we are willing to endure before changing our unworkable habits.

When I was in the deepest depths of my addiction, I was on automatic pilot. I didn't even think about addiction; I just acted. I realize that my DNA, my parents, and many other reasons could be used as justification for why I became addicted, but let's take a moment to examine the facts.

I, alone, picked up a cigarette and put it in my mouth. No one but me drank beer with my friends before, during, and after school. And let's not forget, no one but me purchased and ingested drugs. I took those actions. I repeated those actions. I developed those habits. By taking certain actions repeatedly, and holding true to certain thoughts on how to deal with life's ups and downs, I developed habits that stayed with me long after they became uncomfortable. What started as a pleasurable escape became uncomfortable and grew into pain. When the pain was too great, I looked at the alternatives. Pain is the best friend of change.

Avoidance of Pain Through Character Development

You have now been given an effective way of rapidly changing unworkable beliefs and habits by emotionally choosing what you associate with pain and pleasure. Don't you agree, however, that it would be more enjoyable not to develop poor habits and beliefs to begin with? Are you ready to take responsibility for yourself?

Responsibility: The Ability to Respond

To achieve your full potential, you cannot spend all your time and energy responding to poor decisions. The idea is to raise your consciousness and lower your pain threshold to a point at which you are continuously changing your unproductive habits and behaviors at the first sign of discomfort. Over time, the process becomes easier and almost automatic.

If you are able to make better decisions and develop better habits, you will not be forced to respond as often. In addition, you will avoid much more pain because you'll be developing a better pattern of living in advance of painful situations. Your behavior will adjust itself at the slightest provocation.

You can expedite the process by way of character development, which begins by reducing your participation in the following list of activities: pride, greed, lust, anger, gluttony, envy, and sloth—which are also commonly known as the seven deadly sins. This universally acknowledged list of vices has a long history and evolution throughout the centuries. The first documented list appears in Proverbs and is slightly different from the current form. It was updated and expanded in the fourth century when a monk named Evagrius Ponticus listed what is called "the eight evil thoughts."

Pope Gregory the Great again revised the list of deadly sins, in the sixth century. Dante Alighieri made the list famous in his early fourteenth-century epic poem *The Divine Comedy.* The list in its present order is from the Roman Catholic catechism.

No one wants to feel more pain. By eliminating or at least reducing your participation in any of the activities on this list, you are guaranteed much less pain and much more happiness. Let's examine this list more closely.

Pride

The list of seven deadly sins starts with pride for a reason. Pride, self-justification, narcissism, and vanity all go hand in hand. Pride is considered the most serious of sins especially because it affects the relationship we have with our Creator. After all, it was the pride of Lucifer and his desire to compete with God that caused his fall from grace.

Ego-driven pride leads to selfishness. It tells you that you're justified in your actions, even if it's a lie. It tries to convince you not to examine your motives. Your ego has invented an image of you that it has a vested interest in protecting. Don't let your misguided ego be camouflaged as pride. Your ego will use false pride to keep you from developing this new habit of questioning your motives. Ego-driven, self-justified decisions cause pain to yourself and others. Pride tries to convince you that the rules don't apply to you.

Greed

Unfortunately, greed has become almost celebrated as a virtue in our society. Movies like *Wall Street* tout the advantages of a money-driven existence and the "me-first" lifestyle. Make no mistake: Greed is a reprehensible sickness that warps us into justifying our cravings for overindulgence. Greed is more than hoarding money or material objects. It also encompasses theft, disloyalty for personal gain, bribery, violence, and other less direct forms of manipulation that justify the craving for more.

Lust

Lust is the misguided use of our God-given sexual instincts. Lust is based in selfishness and self-gratification. It is possessive and the antithesis of love. Indulging in prostitution, pornography, sexual addiction, adultery, rape, and incest are examples of lust.

Anger

Anger is often the emotion of last resort when we run out of patience or creative ideas for how to solve problems. Anger ruins our relationships. This wrath manifests itself in uncontrolled feelings of hatred. Rage, revenge, murder, violence, underhandedness, and vengeance are the by-products of anger. Dante described vengeance as "love of justice perverted to revenge and spite." Anger supports the archaic mind-set that might makes right, and whoever yells the loudest, wins.

Gluttony

Gluttony ruins our environment and our health. One look at the condition of our planet or the obesity rate in the modern industrial world shows the fruits of gluttony. Overconsumption to the point of waste is commonplace in our society. The reason that gluttony was considered one of the most deadly sins is that because of the excessiveness and wastefulness of some, others must do without.

Envy

Envy inspires resentment in your heart, which encourages us to undermine others rather than to work toward our own success and fulfillment. Envy is a sickness of the soul that grows out of a hatred of someone else's happiness or good fortune. When you desire to deny others good fortune, you ultimately stifle your own joy.

Sloth

Finally, there is sloth. Sloth is an insult both to our Creator and our fellow human beings. When the seven deadly sins were first written, sloth meant a lack of joy, sadness, and depression. These attributes were considered spiritual apathy and a failure to love God. Sloth shows a lack of gratitude and a misuse of our God-given talents. Through inaction, laziness, and a sense of entitlement, sloth becomes a parasite on the body of humanity. Until you conquer sloth, you will be unable to become successful.

As you look at the list of the seven deadly sins from a sober point of reference, can you honestly say any seem worth indulging in? Whenever you choose to participate in any of these actions, the end result is pain—even if it's just the pain of a guilty conscience. The lower your pain threshold, the less you will indulge in each of these sins. What's interesting is that your ego tells you it will be different next time. It tries to convince you that you won't have to pay the price for your actions. But if you look at it intelligently, the only things you are being asked to give up are behaviors that will ultimately cause you pain anyway.

Your ego tells you that you won't have to pay the price for your actions. But if you look at it intelligently, the only things you are being asked to give up are behaviors that will ultimately cause you pain anyway.

Pain/Pleasure and a Healthy Ego

Many of your problems would fade into nothingness if you could only develop a healthy ego. When you demand too much from others or more material success than you are entitled to, you are setting yourself up for an unhappy experience. If you look back honestly on many of the so-called bad breaks you have suffered, it was most likely self-sabotage via a misguided ego that turned people and situations against you.

Remember the principle we discussed earlier that the mirror reflects back to you what you show the world? How many behaviors listed in the seven deadly sins would you like to have coming toward you? Let's look at some everyday examples:

- When your need to be successful allows you to justify treating others harshly or inconsiderately, they tend to respond to you in the same manner.

- When you act as though you are better than others, you inevitably turn them against you. I am not saying you shouldn't work hard or hold yourself and others to a high standard. What I am saying is that it is much better to be a leader than a boss. People will follow a leader and run from a boss.

- When you have developed an acute sensitivity to people's feelings, a sense of fairness, and an unwavering commitment to your project and your people, on the other hand, you are a true leader. A leader praises in public and corrects in private. A leader doesn't just point out problems and weaknesses but, rather, makes an effort to catch people doing something right. Acknowledging a job well done is very powerful. It takes no great talent to belittle or criticize the workers around you. In the midst of challenging situations, it is the true leader who figures out how to inspire people.

Remember this: To live a life of increase you need the help of others.

I speak for myself when I say that no one ever got the best out of me by treating me poorly. When I felt my worst, they got my worst. If you are in a position of authority, keep your ego in check and stay humble.

The news is filled daily with stories about men and women who lost their way. Many were good folks striving to accomplish big goals. Unfortunately, ambitions and egos led these basically well-intentioned people to misguided choices that eventually brought them crashing back to earth. Their perceived power was too much for them to handle. Somewhere along the way, armed with their newfound power, self-justification crept in and the old values and beliefs that had served them well in the past were cast aside. Values such as honesty, truthfulness, and humility were replaced by pride, greed, and lust.

All of us have seen this scenario play out, whether it is on the national political scene, with a leader in industry, or among friends and coworkers. The result is always the same. When we allow our need for success and happiness to drive us blindly and to justify poor behavior, trouble always follows. Success without happiness is hollow.

The quickest way to achieve a successful and happy outcome is to help others become happy and successful. A question you might ask yourself is this: Where has my need to achieve success caused others pain? I don't ask you this to depress you or to push you to justify your decisions. The purpose of asking this of yourself is to enable you to gain insight into some of the behaviors that are keeping you from achieving abundance. Or, put another way, to encourage you to get into the habit of checking your motives. You can only be as honest with yourself as you are aware. Once aware, you can make better choices about how you want to act.

Many individuals who have achieved sobriety find that something is still lacking from their personal lives. We all have desires for love and sex, for instance. They are God-given and part of our human experience. But once again, our egos and poor choices can open the door to pain and suffering. We have finally hit the tipping point where more marriages end in divorce than survive. Currently in the United States, 52 percent of first marriages and 65 percent of second marriages end in divorce.

Does this statistic apply to anyone you know? Maybe someone you know intimately, like yourself. Perhaps it's time to examine your motives and actions a little more closely. Fear and selfishness are the knockout punches to many relationships. Fear often whispers to our ego, "I am not receiving enough love, time, sex, or money." And selfishness is afraid of losing what it has. Remember, the ego always demands more than it is due, so don't fall into this trap. Ask yourself: What roles have my own fear and my own ego played in my relationship problems?

Keep in mind that you get what you give. To love is to give of yourself—not halfheartedly or selfishly but lavishly. Don't be too quick to give up on the person you married or your significant other. Try something different. Speak the truth to your loved ones. No one likes to be manipulated. Manipulation causes hurt and resentment, which always reflect back to you.

Many people run when the going gets tough. Quite often they run straight to a new relationship. The problem is they bring themselves with them. What I mean by this is they bring the same old insecurities, fears, and resentments to the new relationship. I hear it all the time: "I never pick the right partner. I have bad luck in relationships." Listen, if you don't like the results you are getting, start taking different actions. Until you deal with your own issues, nothing around you will change. You change and then your situation changes; it's not the other way around. No one can make you happy, only you can.

Until you deal with your own issues, nothing around you will change. No one can make you happy, only you can.

Part of the challenge we face is simply that we're living in the twenty-first century where the speed at which we develop new technologies grows faster every day. We want everything fast and we want it done yesterday. This causes us to place unrealistic expectations on others and ourselves. Unfortunately, we often confuse the time that is required to become successful, or the process needed to develop lasting relationships, with a painful or uncomfortable experience.

The need for instant gratification is a relatively new phenomenon. Before electricity, flight, computers, and modern technology, everything was done by humans, and humans are slow. Can you imagine the amount of time it took to grow your own food or to manually chop down trees to build your home? We forget that this was commonplace in North America and Europe just a hundred years ago. It still is in much of the world today.

Nowadays, with the flip of a switch, we can turn the blackness of night into day. With lightning speed, we communicate with people around the world via the phone and the Internet. And let's not forget fast food. Whether it's McDonald's or the microwave oven, we want it and we want it fast.

This same need for instant gratification is partly responsible for the boom in cocaine sales in the 1980s and 1990s. Why waste time drinking or taking a pill when you can get high instantly by snorting cocaine? Today, crystal meth and new designer drugs are even faster acting and longer lasting than cocaine. Even self-destruction has become more technologically advanced.

Being sober can also bring with it a certain expectation for instant gratification. We have all heard of the pink cloud that sometimes accompanies early sobriety. Many people believe that a year of sobriety should also bring success in business and life, and when the armored truck filled with money doesn't back up to their door, they become depressed. But don't be fooled. A successful life, much like sobriety, is built one day at a time over an extended period.

For example, how did you get sober? Studies have proven that it takes as little as twenty-eight days to break a habit and ninety days to create a new one. Do you think it's a coincidence that drug rehab programs usually last twenty-eight days? Or that it is suggested to any newcomer to a twelve-step program that he or she attend ninety meetings in ninety days? As far as I am aware, no one ever was struck sober; it was a process of adopting better habits for an extended period of time. Longer commitments produce enduring results.

These numbers hold true for any habit you are trying to break or any new habit you are trying to create. It's not just for quitting drugs and alcohol. What this means is that if you can discipline yourself for a relatively short period of time, you will greatly improve your life.

Rather than expecting instant gratification, try something different. Try to take joy in every day. One definition of the word *joy* is calm delight. Successful living, which includes not only wealth accumulation but also healthy relationships and peace of mind, is a process. The idea is not to race to the end, but to enjoy the ride. It takes time and self-discovery. It takes a plan of action, as well as the ability to act. It means developing an acute sensitivity to the results you are getting from your actions, and then making the proper adjustments for a better result next time. Of course, it takes perseverance. There are no shortcuts.

The most difficult part about changing is just getting started. But you now know how to get yourself to take action. Associate pain and discomfort with the habit you wish to change and overwhelming joy with the new habit you wish to create. One of the basic laws of the universe is that objects at rest tend to stay at rest, and a body in motion tends to stay in motion. If you have ever tried to move a couch or a dresser, you might have experienced this phenomenon. At first it takes a lot of effort to get the object you are trying to move to budge at all, but once it gets moving, it slides with much less effort. This is the law of inertia. It has been proven that it actually takes much more force to get an object moving than it takes to keep it moving. The hardest part is taking that first step to get the ball rolling.

Once you begin to take action, it is amazing how things tend to fall into place. The law of inertia is a fact that always holds true. Get started and it becomes much easier to keep your dreams moving in the right direction.

Let's Review

- Mankind will endure all types of suffering before becoming willing to change.
- Pain is the best friend of change.
- The easiest way to change a behavior is to associate pain or discomfort with the habit you want to stop and happiness or success with the new habit you are creating.
- You decide what you associate with pain and pleasure.
- The quicker you allow yourself to feel the discomfort of your unproductive habits and beliefs, the faster you will be willing to change. The idea is to lower your threshold for pain.
- Addictions temporarily distract you from reaching this pain threshold and, ultimately, cause you much more pain.
- It's easier to avoid developing bad habits than to go through the pain and discipline of change.

- The seven deadly sins are a universally accepted list of unacceptable behavior. It's unacceptable behavior that leads to pain.
- Your misguided ego separates you from success and happiness. It damages relationships and depletes your earning power.
- There is no shortcut to success. Abundant living is a process. Enjoy the journey.
- Taking the first action toward your new goals is the hardest step but also comes with the biggest payoff.

FULL RECOVERY ACTION PLAN EXERCISES

Now take out your Full Recovery Action Plan and let's get started on the exercises for this chapter.

1. Write down at least two habits you would like to change. The first should involve a personal change you would like to make in your life. It could involve a relationship or an attitude toward your spouse or family. Maybe the habit is health related: perhaps you want to stop smoking or start exercising.

   The second one should involve a career or financial change. You already know how to accomplish this. Write down all the reasons that it would be uncomfortable or painful to continue this bad habit.

2. Part two of this exercise is to write down as many pleasurable, success-driven reasons as you can think of that

> will support creating a new habit to replace the two habits you want to change: personal and career/financial.
>
> Make sure your reasons have as much emotion associated with them as possible. You must be willing to experience a brief amount of discomfort for a short period of time (say, twenty-eight days), but you will ultimately receive the benefit of less pain and more pleasure.

Just as in creating any new habit, your two new habits will take time to develop through constant repetition. Stick with it. Commit your reasons to memory by reading them aloud every day and start practicing perseverance. Start now.

PART II

MOTIVATION

Develop Abundance Awareness

Let us not look back in anger, or forward in fear, but around in awareness.
—JAMES THURBER

DEVELOPING ABUNDANCE AWARENESS involves learning how to remove the mental barriers that prevent you from experiencing a full recovery. Addiction is a disease of selfishness and isolation. Both these traits run counter to abundant living. To develop an abundance awareness, you need to move beyond these carry-overs from the disease of addiction and tap into a power greater than yourself. You have already been blessed with everything you need to create a full and abundant recovery. These traits are built into you. They don't have to be manufactured; you just have to draw them out. Until you realize your oneness with the universe, you will be unable to demonstrate abundance. You might be in possession of money, friendship, education, material possessions, or love and still not be able to recognize or enjoy any of them. Your existence will remain one of separateness and fear until you learn to become aware.

Start today to develop abundance awareness. For most people, this is the beginning of what probably is a new habit. The truth is, you can accomplish any task or acquire any material luxury for which you have a consciousness. (Webster's Dictionary lists consciousness as a synonym for awareness. I think the word *consciousness* is necessary for this discussion because you may be aware of something yet not have the consciousness needed to bring about a demonstration of it.)

To enjoy good health, you need a health consciousness. To be prosperous, you need a prosperity consciousness. To be successful, you need a corresponding success consciousness. To live with abundance, you must have abundance consciousness. You cannot achieve anything beyond your own consciousness. Whatever your circumstances or current situation, it is a projection of your consciousness and your understanding of reality. If you are currently unable to obtain abundance in your life, realize that you must change your consciousness. The outer will not change until the inner is made aware. If you try to change your outer circumstances without a corresponding change of your inner awareness (or consciousness), you may succeed temporarily, but ultimately you will be doomed to failure.

The Bible says in Proverbs, "As a man thinketh in his heart, so is he." Many times this line is misquoted. You hear people say, "As a man thinks, so shall he be." Of course, this statement is a weak substitution.

To "thinketh in your heart" isn't just knowing something intellectually; it means also feeling it with emotion. Thought always precedes action. That's why it's so important to exercise caution when choosing your thoughts. Thought coupled with intense emotion grows into a force of nature.

Effective praying is the process of raising your consciousness to a higher level of awareness. Allowing God to empower your actions is much more effective than relying on your ego or intellect alone. One way of raising your awareness is to focus on a spiritual attribute that you need to develop. You do this by gently meditating on the subject and affirming the unlimited potential the Creator has placed in you. This is a way of practicing the presence of God.

Your ability to receive all good things and raise your awareness is only restricted by the limits you place on God. Try it. Make a conscious decision to hold thoughts of prosperity rather than lack. I know a man whose prayer is, "God, please release me from my own mind." The idea is to release your mind from the past. Think about how good you feel now that money is no longer a problem. Rejoice in feelings of good health. Feel joy for your ability to overcome addiction. Practice walking, breathing, and acting as if the life you desire is happening now. Really feel it! Practicing this daily is important. Training yourself to expand beyond your limited view of self is a process.

The idea is to release your mind from the past. Feel joy for your ability to overcome addiction. Practice acting as if the life you desire is happening now.

As you practice these types of thoughts and actions, the awareness you develop will become reality. When you put emotion behind this kind of thinking, you put your mind and body in a peak state, thus relieving pressure. When you are relaxed and in this peak state, your mind is allowed to expand and create. When you are pressured and living on the hamster wheel in your head, the flow of ideas is stifled. When you are in a positive, joyous state of heightened awareness, the flow of ideas comes naturally.

No doubt you have experienced times when you misplaced something or had to remember a name or a date and the harder you thought about it, the more elusive your task became. However, when you let go and relaxed, or changed your focus, your awareness opened up and the answer just seemed to pop into your consciousness.

On the physical plane, action is needed to accomplish a task. When learning to raise your consciousness, action often actually interferes with the process. The ability to calm yourself and open your mind is essential for the answers to appear.

Raise Your Level of Awareness

There are many techniques for achieving inner peace and raising your awareness. For instance, I have heard of people who sit in a dimly lit room with a pen and paper in hand, listening for ideas. When an idea comes, they write it down. The method doesn't matter. What does matter is that you are at peace. These are habits and new ways of thinking that you can develop in yourself. I promise they will benefit you in all areas of your life. There are many excellent books and publications dealing with the subject of meditation and relaxation techniques to help expand your awareness. I have personally found that improving my abilities in these areas has had a profound and positive effect on my life.

When I find myself on the hamster wheel, going around in mental circles, what works for me is to forget about the problem and turn it over to a power greater than myself. I do my best to put it out of my mind. When I go home at night, I sit in my hot tub and totally relax. Nine times out of ten, the answer to my challenge reveals itself in that setting. How does that happen? I believe it's because when I am totally relaxed and at peace, my awareness expands. I am not talking to myself or keeping my own counsel. I am meditating and listening for the answer.

I have a business partner who also happens to be my father. He is amazed at how many times I have been able to solve a problem by following this simple, proven method. Now, whenever we encounter a major difficulty at work, he actually encourages me to go sit in the hot tub that night! I relax physically and mentally. As I expand my awareness, I allow the collective guidance of the universe to enter my consciousness.

This practice has been used in many different forms and by many different creative thinkers. Thomas Edison was famous for taking twenty-minute catnaps when he was stumped and couldn't figure out what action to take next. It was by this method that he solved the problem with the original incandescent light.

The reason it took ten thousand different attempts to invent the light bulb was that the wire filament in the glass tube would burn up as soon as the electrical current was added. Edison kept substituting different materials (including horsehair) for the wire filament, but nothing worked.

Exhausted one afternoon, he took a nap. As his awareness expanded, he dreamed about a time when he was a boy watching the local men make charcoal. They lit wood on fire and then buried it under dirt, thereby depriving it of oxygen. The wood smoldered for days, eventually compressing and turning into charcoal. Edison awoke from his nap and immediately ran to his lab, where he proceeded to pump all the oxygen out of the glass tube. When he switched the electricity on, the wire filament didn't burn up. Edison had created the first practical electric light bulb.

Edison also dreamed of the phonograph while he was catnapping, but his genius was his ability to take action. Immediately upon awakening, he started turning his dream into reality. Amazingly, it worked the very first time.

Edison was deaf. When asked if he considered his deafness a handicap, he replied that, to the contrary, deafness had been a great help. It had sharpened his awareness. It had saved him from having to listen to a lot of worthless chatter, and it had taught him to hear from within. How's that for turning adversity into a blessing! And his ability to triumph over adversity has blessed us all.

In the creative or the spiritual world, action actually delays our ability to find solutions. All of humanity's greatest accomplishments originally take place in the workshop of the mind. Back to my supercomputer analogy: you introduce a question, challenge, or frustration, and then your mind gives you possible solutions to your question. The key is to be relaxed, at peace, and ready to receive. When the solution is revealed, then it's time to take action.

What Does Abundance Mean to You?

Awareness is only one part of "developing abundance awareness." Abundance is the other part of the equation. It's important to clearly define what abundance means to you.

Abundance is represented by different things to different people. Sobriety is certainly a form of abundance to a person in recovery. To someone serving a life sentence in prison, freedom would probably be viewed as abundance. Offered the choice between the $10 key that opens the cell door or $1 million, most would rather have the key and freedom. Ask a terminal cancer patient if he would take the million or good health.

> It's important to clearly define what abundance means to you.

In the Western Hemisphere, abundance has almost become synonymous with money. Money is only one of the many ways, of course, in which abundance manifests itself. Often people who consider themselves spiritually superior downplay the importance of money in a full recovery. I believe that a sufficient amount of money is an important component in your ability to demonstrate a full recovery. Just as there are spiritual rules that must be learned and practiced to raise your consciousness—and recovery rules that must be observed to enjoy sobriety—there are also wealth rules that must be accepted and practiced to achieve material abundance in a capitalist society.

Capitalism at its best is when people are rewarded according to their contribution, not according to their greed. Let's say you want to earn more money. Did you notice I said earn, not make more money? I live in the USA, and unless you are employed at the US Mint of the US Treasury Department, you can't make money. If you try, you are pretty much guaranteed not to achieve "abundance awareness" but "lack-of-freedom awareness." The federal government frowns on counterfeiters. What this means is you must work and earn money. So the question is, how do you earn more money?

The easiest way to earn more money is to provide others with quality goods and services. You exchange your time, creativity, products, or services for someone else's money. If your product or your service is of better quality, unique, or perceived as a better value than your competitors' products or services, your monetary reward will be greater. This is also known as supply and demand. If there is a high demand for your product or service and a limited supply, people are willing to pay a higher price for it. The quickest way to wealth is to understand this simple principle and stop trying to take shortcuts. You can't make money. You must earn money.

To achieve abundance you must develop abundance awareness. If money and material abundance are what you are seeking, you can start where you are. Begin today acting like the person you want to become. No matter what your position or what business you presently find yourself employed in, there are opportunities for you to prosper and earn even more money. Employers are always looking for ways to increase profits. Start developing the habit of thinking powerful thoughts, asking better questions about your opportunities, and raising your personal consciousness. A key question to ask yourself is, how can I improve someone else's business and get paid for it?

When I first got sober, I was working for a retailer. There I was: fresh out of rehab and making very little money. Every day, customers asked me for items that we did not stock. I could easily have developed an attitude of "who cares?" But I did just the opposite. I started to keep a list of all the items these customers wanted but my store did not carry. The revenue loss from missed sales was thousands of dollars per month. When I presented my list to the store manager, he was impressed and amazed. He contacted the buying office and arranged for the most requested items to be stocked.

Remember the mirror? I contributed more than I was being paid for, and in turn I received more than I had bargained for. I was beginning to develop my abundance awareness.

The results from that simple action were compounded many times over. Not only did I feel great about myself, because I had taken an action to better serve my customers, but I also received recognition from my boss. That one idea separated me from many of the other store employees. Because I had shown initiative, I was given an opportunity to take some management training classes and started my journey up the corporate ladder. By giving more service than I was getting paid for, I started to earn more money. Remember what I said earlier: First you do the work and then you receive the benefit. This is how life really works.

The suggestions in this book work in all circumstances. The same set of principles that I learned in recovery I took into the workplace. And the same lessons I learned on the sales floor of that company I took with me on my journey up the corporate ladder and then into my own businesses. I told you about the affirmations I kept on the fingertips of my right hand that help me change my opinion of me: God wants me sober; God wants me happy; God wants me abundantly wealthy; God wants me spiritually fit; and God wants me to help others.

The same set of principles that I learned in recovery I took into the workplace. The affirmations I kept on my fingertips helped me change my opinion of me.

Let me share with you the ones I kept on my left hand.

Remember, I was working in a retail environment, so they pertain to that job. They went like this: I will be in stock; I will have the shelves downstocked; I will have price signs on all merchandise; I will have clean, working displays; and I will greet every customer with a smile. I figured out that by excelling in the basics on a daily basis, I would become more valuable to my employer. In turn, my employer began to treat me as the asset I was.

I treated all customers as if they were paying my bills because, in actuality, they were. When dealing with a difficult customer, I would imagine them waving hundred-dollar bills at me. It made—and still makes—the situation easier to handle. I started to understand that the Creator gave me certain gifts and abilities that could be used to help me advance my career. I became a problem solver. I also recognized my potential. I saw people in high-paying positions who were no smarter than I was. I began to understand that the universe plays no favorites. If I wanted more abundance in my life, I had to work for it. We all have gifts to be used; we just have to overcome our fear of using them.

Since leaving the corporate world, I have started and operated several businesses. The lessons I learned about asking better questions still apply. It makes no difference if you are selling widgets or building houses; the thought process is the same. In my own business, I'm always seeking ways to develop and implement better quality control and increase customer cultivation. You might ask what I mean by customer cultivation. It means growing or increasing my crop of customers: preferably a crop of customers with a large disposable income. Before I make any changes in my operating procedures, I ask myself a series of questions. It goes something like this:

1. Will the proposed change make it easier for my customers to purchase?
2. Is the change going to save my employees time, which will increase bottom-line profits?
3. Will the change make my employees' jobs easier and more enjoyable, thus increasing morale and possibly productivity?
4. How will the proposed change affect or improve relationships with my suppliers?

If I can answer these and other questions to my satisfaction, I will implement the proposed change. The goal is to always offer better service, develop better relationships, offer quality materials, and of course, as a result, earn more money. Do you have an idea that could save your employer time or money? I have yet to find a successful employer who does not encourage and reward creative thinking from their workforce.

The archaic position of management versus employee must be set aside if we are to survive in a global marketplace. Everywhere in the United States, teamwork, communication, and execution are the new model for successful entrepreneurial enterprises. Organizations, as well as individuals, must develop abundance awareness. If you want an abundant life, always remember you receive in direct proportion to what you give.

The US auto industry is a perfect example of what happens when companies develop abundance awareness and when they lose it. Henry Ford, who helped usher in the industrial age, was not an instant success. His first company went out of business not because he didn't have a good product, but because the manufacturing process involved was too costly and too slow. Following this setback, Ford decided to ask himself a better question: Who already had a proven production method that he could borrow? His answer came from the Chicago slaughterhouses.

At the beginning of the twentieth century, the United States was mainly an agricultural nation. The Chicago slaughterhouses had developed what was called a disassembly line to butcher as many cows and process the meat in the shortest amount of time possible. Ford developed his assembly line by using the same idea in reverse. Using this method Ford's workers dropped production time from twelve hours and 30 minutes per car to one hour and 33 minutes per car. This proved very profitable.

Ford's next move surprised everyone in the business community. He started paying his assembly line workers five dollars per day, which was more than double what comparable workers earned. He had the awareness to recognize that if his workers had more disposable income, they could afford to purchase a car. He turned his employees into customers, and the abundance reflected back to him. Further by-products of this progressive thinking were that he reduced worker turnover, increased worker morale, and attracted a better quality of employee to the company—all of which also grew profits.

Today's US auto manufacturers do not have abundance awareness and have created a climate in which management and employees distrust or sabotage each other. Foreign manufacturers have been taking market share away from the American auto producers for years. There was a time, not so long ago, that the US auto industry was recognized as the world leader, but shortsightedness, greed, and arrogance have allowed competitors to pass them by.

Foreign manufacturers seem to have developed abundance

awareness in the realm of business. They encourage teamwork and reward productivity. The result is a better image and a quality product, as well as increased job security for both employees and management. And of course let's not forget more profit for the stockholders!

The US automakers have begun to see the error of their ways, and I believe they have met and possibly even surpassed foreign automakers from a quality standpoint. However, as a result of years of backward thinking, they still have a lot of image repair to do before they are once again recognized as the world leader.

Remember the mirror? The quickest way to achieve wealth is to help someone else become wealthy. The same principle holds true if you are a manager or a business owner. Henry Ford understood this principle and used it to his advantage. He realized that by helping his employees develop their own abundance awareness, he could become abundantly wealthy.

Consider some of the fastest-growing and most successful companies in the last thirty years: companies such as Walmart, Microsoft, and The Home Depot, among others.

Sam Walton started a small five-and-ten in Arkansas that grew into the largest retail chain on the planet. Bill Gates dropped out of college and started Microsoft with fellow computer enthusiast and high school friend Paul Allen. Bernie Marcus and Arthur Blank were fired from a small hardware chain called Handy Dan. They mortgaged their homes to raise the money to create The Home Depot.

What's amazing is that these people managed to grow their companies from absolutely nothing into some of the largest businesses in the world within just one generation. And each of these men came to be billionaires.

These companies grew to be the biggest and best not just by

providing the excellent goods and services that their customers wanted, but also by making their employees partners in their businesses. Their founders realized that to achieve abundance they had to help others achieve abundance. This was accomplished in part by issuing every employee company stock in the business. To put it simply, a share of stock is a fractional ownership of the business. Everyone from the CEO to the janitor was offered the ability to purchase stock at a discounted price, and in many cases given stock free of charge.

This had an incredible influence on morale, loyalty, productivity, and teamwork. As a stockholder and owner of the company, all employees had a vested interest in the profitability of the business. As owners, they felt an obligation to take care of the customer, ensuring the continued growth of the business. When the company profited, the stock price increased and the employees profited.

Management encouraged suggestions from all employees on how to better serve the customers, as well as to improve employee morale and working conditions. They also promoted employees from the hourly level to the management level rather than hiring management away from competitors. This grew a company culture of teamwork and a sense of possibility. Every worker had the opportunity to advance. This type of teamwork and inclusiveness rewarded everyone handsomely.

During the 1990s, for instance, The Home Depot had more millionaires working for the company than anywhere else on earth. I have personally known parking lot attendants who earned less than $8 per hour who had a net worth in excess of $1 million due to the outstanding performance of The Home Depot's stock.

Now let's follow this company into the next century. The Home Depot, once considered the darling of Wall Street and voted the most admired in America several times by *Forbes* magazine, began to lose focus. They started to regress and lose their abundance awareness. Standards started to slip. Due to both a lack of competition and an accelerating growth rate, the company's management team and employees developed a sense of entitlement. Customer service, which is the lifeblood of any business, began to slip. Management began to fear employees and lawsuits. Holding the line on customer service ended up taking a backseat to avoiding employee-management controversy.

Customers did not appreciate the drop in service. They stopped spending as much money when shopping, which was evidenced by a lower average sale at the cash register. Store managers were put under increasing pressure to grow profits. Payroll was cut. Lower wages attracted a lower-quality, less-committed employee to both the hourly wage earner and the manager level. As profits fell, store managers' stock options and bonuses were reduced, increasing career dissatisfaction. The founding partners retired and a less-committed management team, with a shortsighted vision, filled the vacuum. Greed and arrogance at the senior management level replaced the teamwork and customer cultivation standards that built the company.

To sum it up, the company that was once the most admired in the country simply lost its way. They forgot that employees are living, breathing assets that should never be taken for granted. They are not numbers on a balance sheet. When employees are made partners in a business, compensated fairly and motivated properly, profits increase. The stock that split one to two times per year for over a decade, making many people millionaires, has not had a split in over fourteen years as of this writing. After this long downward trend, the Board of Directors has finally replaced ineffective leadership and has pledged to bring The Home Depot back to its roots.

How did this happen in the short span of thirty years?

The lesson is simple. Never abandon abundance awareness. Everyone in your organization must share an awareness of abundance, from the janitor to the CEO. The customer knows when that awareness disappears because service declines. You get what you give. Remember that the mirror reflects back to you. If you want more, give more. If you want less, take more. If you want to be wealthy, help others become wealthy. Keep in mind that the same rules work in reverse.

Employees, customers, and suppliers are a wealth of knowledge. Ask them for input and you might be surprised what you hear. Weigh all feedback and take the appropriate action. If you don't, your competitors will. That's how capitalism works.

Do you have a desire to start your own business? Are you working in an environment you have outgrown? Have you created a new product you want to bring to market? Then follow your dreams. If you don't, you will never be truly happy. Every product, every business started with an idea followed by an action.

Don't be overwhelmed by the size of your dream. A journey of a thousand miles starts with a single step. Take the first step. Live in the day, just twenty-four hours. Take care of those twenty-four hours and be productive. Do the best you can and leave tomorrow for tomorrow.

Celebrate your successes and learn from your challenges.

Before you know it, you'll be surprised how far you've traveled. God would not have planted the desire in you without giving you the means to accomplish your dreams. Dare to develop your "abundance awareness." Start living in recovery, not just existing in recovery, by constantly and consistently increasing and advancing.

Let's Review

- You cannot achieve anything beyond what your own consciousness will allow.
- Prayer and meditation are essential to the process of raising your awareness.
- A calm mind allows for creativity.
- To truly get what you desire, it's important to define your concept of abundance.
- Money can't be made; it must be earned.
- More service to others equates to more personal success in your own life.
- If you want more, give more; if you want less, take more.

FULL RECOVERY ACTION PLAN EXERCISES

It's time to bring out your Full Recovery Action Plan. You will need five minutes for this exercise. Make sure the TV and stereo are off.

What I want you to do is just sit, close your eyes, and relax. Try doing this for five minutes, uninterrupted. Try not to think of anything. Let your mind go blank. Every time a subject pops into your head, gently turn your focus to the sound of your own breathing. Focus on the slight sensation at the tip of your nose as you breathe in and out. Just concentrate as you inhale and exhale.

If you are like most people it will be very difficult the first time you try this exercise.

Quieting your mind so that the grace of God may enter your consciousness and open your awareness is a learned process. With practice it becomes easier. At first this exercise might seem like the longest five minutes of your life, but if you are able to develop this new habit, you will soon discover it is the secret to self-discovery and peace.

How did you make out with this exercise? Sometimes the hardest thing to do in our fast-paced world is to be quiet and listen for the answers to the problems we face. If you found it difficult, don't beat yourself up. As with any habit, it takes time, practice, and repetition to develop.

Gratitude—Wants—Needs

Gratefulness is the key to a happy life that we hold in our hands, because if we are not grateful, then no matter how much we have we will not be happy—because we will always want to have something else or something more.
—BROTHER DAVID STEINDL-RAST

THE MORTAR THAT BINDS together your foundation for success is "character." It's important to be vigilant and keep close watch on your motives. It's easy to lose focus and let self-justification creep into your consciousness. It's vital to stay true to your ethical values, and nurture strength of character because money and success can be as addictive as any drug.

Peace of mind is a by-product of a clear conscience. Never exchange this peace of mind for profits. If you exchange your peace of mind or your emotional or physical health for money, you definitely paid too much. If money becomes your God, you are truly bankrupt. As I mentioned in earlier chapters, money is important, but it is just a commodity to be exchanged. Money can be replaced very easily over and over again.

Think about how many things are infinitely more valuable than money. For example:

Your health

Your family

Your freedom

Your peace of mind

Your relationship with God

Many people take these priceless gifts for granted. Although they have been given to you for free, all the money in the world cannot replace them.

Gratitude

Excruciating PAIN shooting from my lower back to the tip of my toes as if boiling liquid had replaced the blood in my veins is how it began. This can't be happening, at least not in my good leg. I had been suffering for weeks with back pain, but that was nothing new. Years earlier, I broke several vertebrae in my back and had extensive reconstructive surgery on my right leg, but this latest surprise was happening to my left leg. How could this be? Worst of all, I was in traveling through Georgia and far away from home.

Things went from bad to worse. I became paralyzed in my left leg and foot. I contacted a neurologist in New Jersey who told me to catch the next flight out. Upon landing, I went to his office. After an examination he said I was in immediate need of spinal surgery and that at best I had a 50 percent chance of regaining the movement in my leg. I was rushed into surgery, and thus began a new lesson in patience and gratitude.

I spent the next three weeks in the ICU before being discharged from the hospital. I could not walk and was bedridden for months. All this could not come at a worse time. My son, Rory, and I were scheduled to leave on the trip of a lifetime. It was a white water rafting trip down the rapids of the Colorado River through the Grand Canyon. I had paid for the trip in full and the travel company refused to give me a refund. In addition, I had just started a new business and was not able to even get out of bed, never mind go to work. Things looked bleak.

It took six months of hard work for me to be able to move my foot, never mind walk, but by the following year I was ready for action. Against my doctor's advice I booked another white water trip through the Grand Canyon.

We began our journey with a flight to Las Vegas. After we landed and entered the airport I had a chance encounter with a blind man. He was tall, fit, and judging from his accent, Australian. He explained that he was traveling alone. I offered him some assistance and we parted ways. The next day we took a small plane to the North Rim of the Grand Canyon and to my surprise, my Australian friend was on board, and I found out his name was James. We landed on a dirt runway at a working ranch where we would spend the night before taking a helicopter into the canyon to meet the river guides. It soon became apparent that James was a man of action. That afternoon he went horseback riding with us, helped with the chores, and carried his own backpack. The next morning we boarded the raft and began our journey down the river.

The Canyon is a mystical place and I was on a mystical journey.

The river has some of the world's largest rapids as well as some of the most placid stretches of water you will ever see. Around every corner is a breathtaking vista. Having nothing but time on our hands while being in the company of strangers made for an interesting trip. For example, I noticed that James wore a camera around his neck. When we spoke of the sights, he asked me to tell him which direction we were looking, such as beautiful mesa at one o'clock or large bighorn sheep at six o'clock and then he would snap a picture. When I asked why he took pictures that he would never see, he told me it was to show his friends back home where he had been. James was turning out to be a very interesting man.

Rafting the Colorado is extremely physically demanding. There were many times when both my college-aged athletic son and I were barely able to hold on to the raft, yet James would make it seem easy. His constant laughter as we endured the most severe rapids was a joy to behold. As we got to know each other better, James began to divulge his story. He said he had been born with sight but as a boy was diagnosed with a degenerative eye disease. His father was an eye surgeon in Australia but could do nothing to help him. By the time he was in his teens, he was completely blind. He told me it was horrible. He went into a severe depression and stayed in his bedroom for months in a state of self-pity. One day his father came in his room, threw off his covers, and made the following declaration: "Get out of bed. You are going to be blind for a long time so you better figure out what you enjoy and what you want to do with the rest of your life!" His father refused to let him stay in isolation and got him involved with many different activities. After a while, he decided he liked swimming and started entering competitions. James went on to explain that he was the first blind man to swim the English Channel, the Strait of Gibraltar, and around the island of Manhattan. He is the world record holder in both blind and non blind swimming endurance records of all kinds. When I inquired how he knows which direction he's heading he explained he has a person in a boat who shouts out instructions such as left, right, SHARK! James went on to explain that he made the decision to live his life to the fullest despite his challenges. He was presently on hiatus and traveling the world. He works a full-time job and paid for his trip out of his own money. I found it amazing that he was unaccompanied by any chaperone or guide dog and was taking care of himself. He is the most inspirational man I've ever met.

If I had not had my own health challenges, I would have missed the opportunity to meet James. Every adversity brings with it a greater seed of opportunity. When I arrived home from my trip, I encountered a problem with a business deal that had gone awry in my absence. When I started to get upset, my son, Rory, reminded me, "At least you can see." Oh yeah, gratitude. How it puts challenges in perspective and changes my perception of reality. I think of James often when life challenges me and I start to drift into negativity. I would like to suggest the next time you feel life isn't treating you fairly that you think of James Pittar. To paraphrase a line from James's father, "You are going to be an addict a long time; you better figure out what you enjoy and what you want to do with your life." Once you achieve sobriety, the only limitations you have are the ones you place on yourself and your higher power.

Try living with an attitude of gratitude. When you have gratitude, you are at peace. You are truly present and experience the contentment that comes from enjoying what you already possess. Gratitude is wanting what you already possess and needing no more. Be grateful for what you have and more will be given.

> When you have gratitude, you are at peace. You are truly present and experience the contentment that comes from enjoying what you already possess.

Thank God for your health, for without it, all the money in the world will not bring true happiness. Be grateful for the gift of life. Be grateful for having been born in a free country, where you can still pursue your own dreams.

I often ponder the fact—through no effort on my part, my good fortune—of having been born in the USA at a time of unprecedented abundance, and how lucky I am. I could just as easily have been born in some impoverished Third World country, having to beg for food and being eaten by flies. I had no choice in the matter, yet here I am. Have you ever considered this truth about your own life?

It's easy to fall into the collective mantra and complain about how difficult life is. To complain about how hard we must work to earn a living. We complain because we're judging our wealth by Hollywood standards, rather than Third World standards. The reality is that by most of the planet's standards, and certainly in relationship to history's standards, Americans are a wealthy lot. We have an abundance of food, water, clothing, and housing. Americans have unprecedented freedom and civil rights, as well as the right to practice the faith of our choosing without fear of reprisal. We can control our personal environment with heat and air-conditioning. As a nation, we offer the poorest among us an opportunity to obtain government subsidized food, housing, and health care. Many, even at the lowest socioeconomic levels, own a TV and an automobile.

Yet with all of these blessings, we still find room to complain.

We suffer from depression, obesity, and addiction. We are living in the Prozac generation.

Let's put an end to self-medicating and boldly seize the day! To whom much is given, much is expected. Start today to create the future of your choosing. Make a decision and never look back. Live the life you are craving and stop settling for scraps. Be grateful for what you have been given, as well as for the adversity you have experienced that has yet to be turned into opportunities.

All major religions speak of sin. The biggest sin of all is not fulfilling your God-given purpose. The best way to demonstrate your gratitude is to demonstrate your full potential. Learn to avoid poor habits like wasting your time wishing for what you don't have rather than earning it. Stop making excuses and start pressing forward on your quest for a better life. The Creator of the universe is omnipresent and always available to assist you on your journey. When Moses ascended Mount Sinai, he asked God (who was represented as the burning bush), "What shall I call you?" God replied, "I am that I am." That sums it up. I am all things, all time, always omnipresent . . . the beginning and the end.

Remember to focus your gratitude on the creative energy that is responsible for your blessings. Don't ever confuse your career, your government, your money, or anything else as the true source of power. There is only one source of power: that source is God. All other misconceptions of power are ego-based and temporary. The only constant is God. Believe in the power of prayer, which is speaking to God. Practice meditation, which is listening for the answers. When the answers come, take fearless action and don't look back.

For me, the realization that I am not alone has given me the courage to live my destiny. God is closer than my breath and without Him I am nothing. True wealth is the ability to live my destiny without fear.

I have had the opportunity to meet many wealthy people who unfortunately spend much of their lives worrying about losing their fortune. Some are miserly, others angry, some just depressed and fearful. To live such an existence is the opposite of wealth. Fear of poverty, while possessing great wealth, is a hell of one's own making. Rather than being grateful for all they have been afforded, they selfishly cling to what never made them happy in the first place. True wealth is the freedom of knowing, at a gut level, that fundamentally all is well.

My struggles with addiction were a hell of my own making. Rather than having gratitude for all that had been given to me, I chose to squander my time and energy on excess. I called it partying, but it was self-destruction on a grand scale.

Today, I choose not to self-sabotage. I choose to be grateful for what I have and what I don't have. I accept life on life's terms. I take action toward fulfilling my dreams rather than wishing blindly or blaming others for my circumstances.

One simple way of changing my focus is to write a list of everything I'm grateful for in my life.

I am not suggesting that I never feel down or that I'm always upbeat and positive 100 percent of the time. What I am saying is that when I find myself drifting into negative, unproductive thinking patterns, I immediately change my focus. One simple way of accomplishing this is to write a gratitude list. I write a list of everything I'm grateful for in my life:

1. The first thing on my list is always sobriety, for without sobriety I will lose everything else anyway.
2. I'm grateful for my relationship with a God of my understanding.
3. I'm grateful for my health, and the simple things I take for granted like two eyes, ten toes, or the ability to speak.
4. I'm grateful for my wife and son, my mom and dad, my brother and his family, and all my in-laws.
5. I'm grateful for my dog, Butch; my cat, Mr. Bo Bo; and my horses.
6. I'm grateful for the food in the refrigerator and the home where I live.
7. I'm grateful for all my successes and even all my challenges.

I can go on and on, but you get the idea. The things for which I am most grateful haven't changed all that much over the years. To be sober, free, and loved is real wealth that is definitely obtainable by us all. Anyone can create such a list. When you realize all the gifts you have in your life, it's hard to stay unhappy.

I know someone who keeps a gratitude list in a folder that is filled with particularly troublesome legal issues he became involved with as an active alcoholic. The issues are ongoing, and the folder gets opened every couple of months. He keeps the list in with his legal papers to remind him of all the gifts he has been given and to stay grateful. When dealing with the wreckage of his past, he sometimes gets upset, so he takes out his gratitude list and changes his focus.

Maybe you are dealing with an ongoing financial problem or health issue. Keep your gratitude list with your papers and use it to help you change your focus when you become overwhelmed. When you change your focus, you change your reality. For example, when you are angry or you hold on to a perceived injustice or resentment, you keep yourself emotionally tied to the person or situation that's bothering you. You continually relive the pain over and over again. If you repeat this process long enough, you lose the ability to separate your feelings from your idea of who you are.

When you complain about your aches and pains to yourself or others, you take ownership of them. You anchor them into your subconscious. You lose the ability to separate yourself from your aches and pains. You become John with aches and pains, instead of just John. When you put yourself down and claim triumphantly that nothing good ever happens to you, or bad luck is your only luck, it's like cementing that unwanted attribute into your being. Once those thoughts are introduced with emotion, your mind tries to figure out a way to turn them into reality. Thought precedes action. Whatever you focus on consistently with emotion, you will receive.

Remember what God said to Moses: simply, "I am that I am." This statement allows for unlimited potential and does not box God into any one thing we can label. You are not John with aches and pains or John with no luck . . . you simply are who you are: unlimited potential, a child of God.

There is a way to look at this concept from another angle as well. When you say you are John the plumber, and one day you lose the ability to work, have you lost your identity? If you are not a plumber, who are you? If I am Mary, the most beautiful woman in town, and I lose my beauty due to age or an unfortunate accident, who am I? I am probably a very devastated human being. By identifying with these outside labels we limit our potential and set ourselves up for a crisis that can potentially cripple our lives. If John and Mary never let their egos identify with a label, they might not have to experience the debilitating depression that goes along with losing whatever it was the label was based on.

Would it not be better to identify with more intangible character traits like these: I am Mary, a generous, giving person who does my best to help others succeed? Or I am John, who lives my life to the fullest every day? Or how about, I am a child of God, with the potential to overcome any adversity? While these are still labels, we at least leave the ball in our court, never allowing outside forces to dictate who we are or what we can accomplish.

Remember the principle we discussed earlier that the mind is a valuable recovery tool? Whatever you think will eventually manifest itself in your life. Your thoughts determine who you are and how you live.

This is another example of an unbreakable law that is no different from those that govern gravity or mathematics. When I drop an object on the planet Earth, it goes down and never goes up; that's why it is an unbreakable law. The angles of any triangle when added together always equal 180 degrees; it makes no difference what kind of triangle it is. Now, I can't see gravity and I didn't figure out the mathematical principles that always hold true. Nonetheless, I do accept them as principles and they always work. They are constant and unchanging.

The same holds true for the principles that you become whatever your thoughts make of you, and whatever you direct your focus toward will eventually manifest in your life. Instead of arguing with these principles, it's much easier to accept them and use them to your advantage.

It makes about as much sense as arguing the existence or nonexistence of a higher power just because it can't be seen. I can't see gravity either, but it exists, regardless. Gravity is not changing to meet my needs. I can't see my higher power, but his handiwork is all around me and undeniable.

These truths may be hard for some to accept, especially in our modern, politically correct world, but they are truths nonetheless. To quote Socrates, "Truth is its own reward." When you embrace the truth that you become what you think about, you understand the importance of intelligently choosing the thoughts you allow to enter your mind. Choose to stay grateful for what you have and you will know peace of mind.

Wants

Many people say they want something, such as wealth, and then focus on something that is the opposite of earning wealth. They want a big bank account, yet they focus on how impoverished they are, the declining stock market, or the inability to pay their bills. They live in the problem rather than the solution. They want more money, but they don't want to work harder. They want to advances in their careers, but they decide to stay out all night partying or sleep till noon. They want success, but they don't take the actions that lead to success.

Get in the habit (once again, a habit is a learned skill that becomes almost automatic through repetition) of immediately changing or substituting a new thought whenever you find yourself focusing on something you don't want. First change your thoughts, and then take a different action.

Would you like to be a certain type of professional and earn a large salary or are you just daydreaming? Are you willing to invest the time needed to get an education, learn more about your business, and achieve that goal, or are you better at making excuses? It is written in the Bible, "A double-minded man is unstable in all his ways." It does not say in some of his ways; it says in all of his ways. It is in your nature to act rather than to be acted upon. All too often, we find ourselves pulled in two different directions. We want a loving relationship, but we also want to flirt with the opposite sex as much as possible. We want a great and rewarding career, but we want to work as little as possible. It's time to get off the fence. When you're sitting on the fence, all you achieve is a sore backside.

Let's start right now. It's time to figure out what you want. The idea is to decide what you want, get focused, and stop wishing for things that are not in harmony with your main objective. Full recovery is all about achieving abundance, and abundance is whatever you choose it to be. The ability to accomplish your task will be made exponentially easier when you decide exactly what you want and align yourself with the creative force, which for lack of a better term, we call God. This omnipresent being is there to help you overcome fear and develop the strength of character needed for pressing forward.

Many people consider money or wealth to be the ultimate expression of abundance. They feel that if they could just get their hands on enough money all their problems would disappear and life would be wonderful, even though we witness time and again that this is not necessarily so. Take rock star Kurt Cobain as an example. Here is a man who had more money, fame, and success than anyone could need or want, yet because of his self-loathing and addiction he still found it necessary to put a shotgun in his mouth and pull the trigger.

The problem is not money or lack of money. The problem is with the way you think, the way you talk to yourself, the types of conversations and inner dialogue you have with yourself all day long.

Perhaps you believe money is what you want. If you don't have as much money as you want, you have to change the way you think about money. Someone once told me that money is like sunshine . . . there is more than enough for everyone on the planet. If I stand in the sunshine, there is more than enough left for you. It doesn't get depleted. Perhaps you hold the opinion that if you could get your hands on enough money, all your problems would disappear.

You may think you want more money, but after working through the list of questions I pose to you in the next paragraph, you might realize you are looking for something completely different. For example, I know wealthy people who have no free time. They are working their lives away, not enjoying any of the money they have accumulated. They are still accumulating money they will never spend and don't have a clue why.

Write down the answers to the following questions in order to better understand what you truly want.

- Would you rather have money or free time?
- Would you rather have peace of mind or adventure?

- Would you rather have power or anonymity?
- Would you prefer fame or love?
- Would you like to be single or have a family?
- Would you choose good health or unlimited travel?
- Would you rather be sober or own a successful business?
- Would you rather have an education or friends?

When you have finished answering all of the questions, start down the list again and take the answer you chose for each question and create a new question. For example, if your answer to the first question is money, and your answer to the second question is adventure, create the new question, would you rather have money or adventure? Keep repeating this process until you only have one answer left, and that is what you really want. That is what is most important to you.

What do you want? If you don't know what you want, you have little chance of getting it. If you aim for nothing, you will most surely hit your target.

You might be thinking: I want to be married or I want to have a family. Is that what you really want, or do you just want what you think a relationship will give you? Things like security, peace of mind, and structure. Write down a list of what you think you would like to have in your life. Ask yourself, why do I want these things?

> If you don't know what you want, you have little chance of getting it.

Do you want to own a business, or do you want the prestige you believe it will give you? It's time to make some distinctions. When you fearlessly check your motives, you may discover that many of the things you say you want, you really don't want at all.

You might say you want children, for example. Ask yourself why. Do your friends have children and you want to fit in? Do you want to share your love with someone or do you want to receive it? Are you lonely? Does your religion demand it? Do you want to continue your bloodline? Why do you want children?

Do you want material things? Do you want a new Ferrari or an expensive piece of jewelry? Do you want a large home or estate, or do you just want to be envied? Maybe you want to be considered successful. Think about what you want and write it down. Then ask yourself why.

Whatever thoughts you consistently and emotionally hold in your mind will eventually manifest on the material level.

Needs

I have discovered that I'm more motivated by sharing a working truth and helping others learn the principles of recovery and success than I am interested in collecting pictures of dead presidents on paper, which, at the material level, money is.

My need to share my success with my loved ones by providing them with a nicer quality of life provides more motivation for me than the need to increase the size of my bank account. Another thing I have realized is that peace of mind is always a by-product of sharing my success with my loved ones.

We all have a need for water, food, shelter, security, and love. These impulses are hardwired into us to ensure the survival of our species. Most people are aware of these needs. What you might not know is that following these basic needs is one of the greatest human needs of all: the need to be recognized as important among our peers. How you answered the questions on wants gives you clues regarding what type of recognition you are seeking.

Say, for example, adventure was high on your list. You might find yourself seeking acceptance or recognition through skydiving or white water rafting. If education is paramount, you might be interested in pursuing your doctorate. If family was on the top of your list, you might want several children. The point being that each category represents more than it appears to represent. Each represents a form of self-expression through which you seek recognition and fulfillment.

How you answer questions about what you want gives you clues regarding what type of recognition you are seeking.

Often as we mature and grow, our wants and needs change. The importance of certain activities increases or decreases over time as our outlook and priorities change. For instance, at one time owning the nicest Harley-Davidson motorcycle was an all-consuming passion I placed over most things in my life. Today, I can appreciate the artistry and hard work someone invests in their motorcycle, but the Harley has fallen off my list. As of late, sharing what I've learned about a full recovery with others has become increasingly important, and I am absolutely reaping the benefits.

I've been told that the three motivating needs in a person's life are love, sex, and money. This may or may not be true depending on the person. That being said, if you want more of each, I suggest sharing more of each. If you can focus your energy on one goal that combines all three, you will practically be guaranteed of a successful outcome.

I love my wife. Our sexual relationship is giving, caring, and healthy. My desire to give her the finest lifestyle I can motivates me to be more creative in my approach to success and happiness. This is an example of combining all three of my most basic needs. For me, this way of living is much more inspiring than focusing on money alone.

⁂

Gratitude changes your reality by revealing the peace of mind derived from contentment. The ability to take joy in what you already possess calms your mind and exposes you to your true self, allowing the mind to expand and be creative. Gratitude keeps you focused on the present moment.

A life of undisciplined wants robs you of your life energy. You are always focused on fulfillment in the future or regretting missed opportunities in the past, which keeps you from enjoying the present. When thinking about what you want, make sure you check your motives. Always ask yourself the reasons why you want whatever you determine you want.

Accumulation for its own sake will never satisfy your core needs. Trying to satisfy your core needs with an abundance of materialism is just doing more of what never worked to begin with. Our needs are hardwired into us. When you figure out your needs, your wants will take care of themselves. When your needs and wants meet on common ground, you will know peace.

Let's Review

- Gratitude shifts your focus from negative thought patterns to thoughts that are positive, thankful, and joyous.
- Changing your focus ultimately changes your reality.
- Health, family, spirituality, and peace of mind are priceless and free.
- Stay off the fence; decide what you want and get focused.
- Wants are many, but needs are few.
- Never confuse the means with the ends.

FULL RECOVERY ACTION PLAN EXERCISES

Take out your Full Recovery Action Plan and do the following exercise:

Write a list of at least five things you are grateful for in each of the following areas of your life:

Spiritually
Materially
Physical health
Personal relationships

You may be of the mind-set, "I don't have anything to be grateful for." I hope that isn't the case, but if it is, start with the easy topics such as being grateful for your health. Are you lucky enough to be able to see the sunset or a small child? Perhaps you are able to walk or, even better, to run. Do you have a home or a family? How about a job? Did you eat today?

These may seem like very trivial things to be grateful for until you realize that many people on this planet live in substandard housing, with no health care, and go to bed hungry at night. Perhaps you are sober today or haven't had a cigarette; surely you could be grateful for that. Maybe you have just made a decision to try to get sober or to start exercising. This newfound awareness is definitely something for which you could be grateful.

After you have finished your list, ask yourself two more questions:

- With whom can I share my gifts?
- What am I searching for beyond money?

Now it's time to figure out what you want. Write down the topics from the list that follows and arrange them from most important to least important. Some items on the list might seem the same, but if you think about it they're different. For example some people have a job; others have a career. All of the categories might not apply to your situation, so feel free to add or subtract as you see fit.

Arrange the list in order of importance to you and you will be well on your way to discovering what you truly want.

Recovery
Travel
Religion
Money
Spouse
Job
Adventure
Children
Education
Spirituality
Free time
Success
Career
Health
Philanthropy
Friendship
Power
Security
Fame
______________________________ (Fill in the blank)

When you are finished, ask yourself, why do I want this? There are no right or wrong answers. Asking yourself *why* you want what you want will help you understand what is really important to you. Make sure you write the date on your list; that way when you review it over the years, you will be able to chart your progress.

⁂

So, how did you make out with your list of wants? Were you able to make any distinctions between what you thought you wanted and what you actually want? Is it money you want or is it the freedom money brings, the education it pays for, or the ability to help those less fortunate?

You can see it's easy to confuse the means with the ends. The money/wealth is the means; what you want to do with it is the ends. It's much easier to keep pressing ahead with the acquisition of money when you place a heavy focus on the reasons for acquiring it.

One basic human need is to be recognized as important by our peers. What do your wants reveal about the recognition you are seeking?

Are your wants and needs in harmony with one another?

Write down one core need that is not currently being fulfilled, and one action step you can take today to fulfill it. It might be as simple as making a phone call. The important thing is that you take action.

I would like to end this exercise with a question you would do well to answer every day: What can I do today that will improve my relationships and increase my commitment to my God, my loved ones, and my country?

Live Inspired

If your actions inspire others to dream more, learn more, do more, and become more, you are a leader.
—JOHN QUINCY ADAMS

MANY PEOPLE in recovery today are merely the walking dead. They have lost their confidence, buried their dreams, cremated their ambitions, and settled for an empty, mediocre existence. They reside in cemeteries of their choosing. These cemeteries are surrounded with fences made of conformity, littered with headstones bearing names such as doubt and fear. When you submit to conformity and don't pursue your God-given creative desires, something inside of you dies.

You've probably heard the story of how Jesus raised Lazarus from the dead. The miracle is that by an act of faith and fearlessness you, too, can be raised from the dead. You were not created to live an uninspired, mediocre life.

The word *inspired* is often used to describe a person who has accomplished some great task or achieved a level of success. *Webster's Dictionary* defines *inspired* as "outstanding or brilliant in a way or to a degree suggestive of divine inspiration"; a divine influence or action on a person held to qualify him to receive and communicate sacred revelation is the definition of inspiration. This definition confirms that your higher thoughts come from God.

The ability to fulfill your desires is hindered only by your ability to receive God's grace. The Creator has the ability to grant you any spiritual or material thing you desire. What limits you is your understanding of how to receive them. It would be as if the Creator were a television satellite circling Earth, sending out signals across space and time, and you did not own a receiver.

It makes no difference whether you call it your soul, your mind, or your spirit; the truth of the matter is you *do own a receiver.* What usually happens, though, is that through lack of focus or unawareness, you have it tuned to the wrong station. What's worse is that sometimes you choose to turn your receiver off because you don't want to hear the message.

The reason you don't pursue your dreams is fear. Let me repeat something from earlier: You can only be as honest as you are aware. When you choose not to turn the receiver on, it's because you know that once you are aware, you are responsible. Once you are responsible, you are accountable. For this reason, some feel it's easier to remain unconscious than to take action and risk being disappointed. Unfortunately, this keeps you from experiencing all the grace the Creator has to give.

I would like you to think back to when you were a small child. The world was an exciting place to be explored and enjoyed. You had no fear. You tried everything, never really concerned about the outcome, just craving new experiences. You knew no limits.

Then something happened to change your outlook. Parents, relatives, teachers, TV, and society as a whole started leaning on you and grabbing for your attention. They begin to apply pressure. Through repetition they convinced you of what's good and acceptable and of what's bad and unacceptable. You got trained just like Pavlov's dogs. When you conformed, you were called "good." You were given praise and shown love. When you didn't conform, you were called "bad." You were shunned and experienced a sense of separation from the source of love. The question I have for you is this: How do you know the rules or beliefs you have been conforming to are the right way for you to live?

The Downside of Nonconformity

Nonconformity can be an asset when used intelligently. Just keep in mind, however, that the same character traits that can lead us to the mountaintop when properly used can also lead us to the gutter when misused.

I thought that by doing drugs I was being a nonconformist. In reality, I was conforming to the worst aspects of society. I thought that drinking and drugging provided me with the inspiration to see what people in the straight world could not see. This was false inspiration.

When we achieve sobriety, we sometimes lose our motivation. Drugs and alcohol, and the quest for drugs and alcohol, motivated our actions. This is not inspiration. Without that drive, misguided as it is, we sometimes feel uninspired. We settle for something less than our dreams. We accept a mediocre life.

The Upside of Nonconformity

To achieve a full recovery and move beyond the mediocre requires fearlessness and inspiration: the fearlessness to find a higher power of your understanding, and the faith needed to be inspired by and follow its leading. For full recovery, we have to be willing to be nonconformists once again, but this time we'll be true nonconformists who are achieving their God-given destiny. True nonconformists have accomplished many of the greatest achievements in human history.

> To achieve a full recovery and move beyond the mediocre requires fearlessness and inspiration.

The Wright brothers succeeded in inventing the machine that enabled people to fly. Prior to their success, however, they were scorned and told that if humans were supposed to fly, they would have been born with wings. As a result, Orville and Wilbur carried out most of their experiments and test flights in secret to avoid unwanted attention.

Christopher Columbus was considered mad because he thought the world was round. He was told he was going to sail right off the end of the Earth.

Galileo, the famous Italian astronomer, was persecuted by the Catholic Church for his belief in heliocentrism—the theory that the sun is the center of the universe. The Catholic Church of the sixteenth century taught geocentrism, which states that Earth is the center of the universe. Galileo was right, but church leaders labeled him a heretic because his theory conflicted with their literal interpretation of scripture.

The church leadership was not about to acknowledge anything or anyone who could possibly challenge their authority by disproving any of their teachings. The church taught that you needed to obey their rules. The church taught that it was the only acceptable medium for contact with God. If you want to go to heaven, if you want to be saved, you'd better conform.

Let's not forget the most famous nonconformist of all, Jesus Christ. Whether you consider Jesus the Son of God, a prophet, a religious zealot, a revolutionary, or just a man who was a carpenter, you must acknowledge that he is the most influential and most talked and written about person to ever walk the earth. At the time of Christ's life, his ideas and actions were the most nonconforming, revolutionary way of thinking the world had ever known. And in many ways, they still are today. In the Sermon on the Mount, Christ taught us, "Judge not, that you be not judged. For with what judgment you judge, you shall be judged: and with what measure you mete, it will be measured to you again."

He also told us, "Resist not evil: but whosoever shall hit you on thy right cheek, turn to him the other also . . . love your enemies, bless them that curse you, do good to them that hate you, and pray for them which despitefully use you, and persecute you."

Christ commanded us to forgive one another. Christ lived and did his greatest works and miracles among the poor and outcasts of society. He ministered to the lepers, prostitutes, and thieves, as well as to the tax collectors and people in power. His example of forgiving his persecutors, "for they know not what they do," is still revolutionary two thousand years later.

Many call themselves Christians today, but remember: we are defined not by our intentions, but by our actions. Emerson put it this way: "What you are shouts so loudly in my ear that I cannot hear what you say."

Humanity owes a debt to these nonconformists and many other courageous men and women who followed the dictates of their consciences and bucked the system, resisting the easier, softer way of conformity. They have changed our world for the better. They chose to live at a higher level of awareness. They did not cower before the masses.

The Serenity Prayer says, "God grant me the serenity to accept the things I cannot change, the courage to change the things I can, and the wisdom to know the difference."

It's easy to hide behind the "acceptance of things I cannot change" part of the prayer. You hear it all the time: "I have to learn to accept everything, now that I'm in recovery." Or, "I must learn to accept people, places, and things."

But the prayer also states we need "the courage to change the things we can." Some things need to be changed. That's when wisdom becomes necessary. It takes wisdom to guide you through the process. That is where your sponsor, teacher, or spiritual guide can help you on your journey. Show some backbone and courage. Help change yourself and our world for the better. Show the courage to open your mind to a new level of possibility.

The human mind is often compared with fertile soil. The Bible says in Galatians, "Whatsoever a man sows, that shall he also reap."

Be careful as to the thoughts you plant in your mind. Whatever seeds or thoughts you cultivate will bear fruit. If you continuously plant the same old thoughts, you will receive the same old results. You can't plant corn and expect to grow mushrooms. If you choose not to plant anything, your fertile soil will grow weeds.

The same is true of your mind. You must constantly care for your mind. Pull out the weeds and fertilize it with good ideas if you want it to return an abundance of crops. Whatever you plant in your mind will grow. Plant the seed; let God do the work.

We all have been subjected to rules, affirmations, and concepts that have been allowed to take root in our subconscious minds that are, at best, suspect. Some of these ideas are lies, others are fears, and others are simply incompatible with the person's God-given demeanor. Yet through repetition and, finally, acceptance, these ideas become part of your personality traits. Having all these incompatible rules and emotions rattling around in your head, coupled with the feeling of not living your destiny, leads to confusion and anxiousness. Is it any wonder people seek escape?

Nowadays, it has become popular in the medical community to blame all sorts of addictions on our DNA. I believe the reason people become addicts is far deeper than DNA, even though DNA plays a part. I believe it's because we don't feel comfortable in our own skin. We aren't happy with who or what we are. We lack self-esteem, so we attempt to change our state or feelings by using our drug of choice. When I say drug I mean alcohol, narcotics, food, gambling, work, sex, or whatever unhealthy distraction we choose. As strange as it may sound, some people are addicted to failure, depression, and self-sabotage.

Our jails today are overflowing with men and women who are permanently condemned to the life of a convict and the merry-go-round of the judicial system. Granted, many are self-destructive, some are violent, others insane; if you trace the problem back to its roots, however, you'll find that a lack of self-esteem and a lack of a true spiritual connection have led them down this path. Lack of self-esteem mutates into lack of self-respect, and this cycle is costing us all plenty.

As a society, it's popular to be tough on crime. We love to punish, only we call it justice. As of late, the line between justice and vengeance has become increasingly fuzzy.

Remember the mirror? Everything reflects back to you. If a person was never taught self-respect, he or she is not capable of giving respect to anyone else. You cannot give away what you don't have. If people believe they are being punished unjustly, they will act the same toward others. It's an endless cycle.

In the United States, one-third of the federal government is known as the legislative branch. Their sole purpose for existence is to create new laws. Obviously, they take this job very seriously. But the result is an overabundance of laws and strict punishment for nonconformity. We are shoehorning more and more people into an uncomfortable fit. Political correctness, once touted as a way of showing respect for all, has been used as a club to stifle self-expression. If you think or act differently from the masses, you are considered weird or incorrigible.

It starts at a very young age. It's popular nowadays for parents and schools to medicate high-energy or type A personality children. We are giving Ritalin and other mind-numbing, impulse-controlling drugs to the next generation of innovators and entrepreneurs. It's disgusting, and shows the lengths to which society is willing to go to deal with nonconformity.

When I think back on my childhood and some of the subject matter I was taught in school, it's amazing I didn't burst right out of my skin. The lessons and the way they were presented was so boring, it's no wonder the teachers couldn't hold my attention. I thank God drugs were not passed out to children when I was young because I certainly would have been a candidate. We should nurture creativity and encourage fresh thinking instead of medicating our future leaders.

Medication is not the only way for dealing with high-energy boys and girls. Why don't we start the school day with gym or some other physical activity and kill two birds with one stone—seeing as there's also an obesity problem among the youth in our country? Let the kids have some exercise and run off some excitement before they start their school lessons for the day. Mindfulness as practiced in meditation and yoga is also a wonderful way to lessen anxiety and achieve balance. Not only will they be healthier, but they also will be more able to concentrate.

As we age we encounter more and more societal pressures upon us to conform. All this pressure for success and conformity produces is a universal sickness known as anxiety. Over time, anxiety grows into inferiority because we are not meeting expectations. Guilt develops from being a disappointment to others and oneself. Eventually, it's too much for us and we seek escape. Thus begins the habit of self-medicating.

This works only temporarily, until it turns into addiction. Now we have a new set of problems. Not only are we anxious and uncomfortable, our addiction often causes us to make irrational decisions. We lose our ability to deal with life on life's terms. We isolate. We begin to show up in hospitals and rehabs. And for many of us, we end up being removed from society. The long journey that started with anxiousness and nonconformity culminates with the ultimate insult—jail.

As a society, we think nothing of incarcerating people for years on end. Let's examine the results. The latest US Justice Department statistics state that one out of every forty-four people in this country is in jail. One out of every four people incarcerated on the planet earth lives in the United States of America. The United States has a per capita incarceration rate five times higher than the average of all countries worldwide. If you take into account the statistics for people in other types of correctional supervision programs, which includes home incarceration, parole, and probation, the number increases to one out of every thirty-one people is incarcerated or being supervised by the Department of Corrections. The United States is known as the land of the free and the home of the brave, but the numbers as of late don't bear it out. These statistics shout out fear.

One of the fastest-growing businesses in the United States over the past thirty years has been prison construction. What's interesting is that the current justice statistics show that 48 percent of all drug arrests in the country last year were for marijuana possession. In addition, 60 percent of all people incarcerated in state prisons who were serving time for drug possession had no history of violence. Statistics also show that better than 90 percent of the people in jail were high on either alcohol or drugs when they committed their offense. All told, four out of five drug arrests are for possession, not dealing, and most of the dealers arrested are the low-level street variety, not the billionaire drug cartel leaders who profit from this endless procession of misery. When you see the statistics, it's easy to conclude that we waste untold lives and billions of dollars on a system that doesn't work.

I know a couple, Fred and Pat, who specialize in picking men and women off the junk heap of life. Fred deals mainly with repeat drug offenders. Many men come directly from jail to his establishment. Fred teaches them through discipline, mentoring, and caring how to be productive members of society. Fred has been doing God's work for more than twenty years. Fred's students have an 87 percent success rate. That means if you graduate from his program, you have an 87 percent chance you will never see the inside of a prison again. In addition, you will leave with enough self-esteem and self-respect to never drink or drug again.

Not everyone graduates. Some choose not to complete the program, but these are incredible statistics nonetheless. These men and women work and contribute to the cost of their own treatment. Typically, the student's rehabilitation lasts twelve months. The cost not covered by the earnings of the student averages $25,000 per person, which is made up by grants and donations. The graduates become productive members of society.

Now let's compare these results with our present prison statistics and see how much value we are getting for our tax dollars. It costs more than $38,000 a year to keep someone locked up in a system that doesn't work, and there is a 90 percent chance the person will commit another crime and end up back in jail. If the person is at a maximum-security prison, the cost exceeds $56,000 a year. These figures don't take into account the fact that the prisoner will probably be back in jail after a relatively short period of time, compounding the waste of taxpayer dollars.

Jim's Journey to Full Recovery

I'm going to share another story; this time it's about a man I'll call Jim to protect his anonymity. What's more important than his name is his miraculous recovery. Jim is a business associate. His story is a fairly common one with an uncommon outcome.

Jim started experimenting with drugs and alcohol in high

school, and like many others, he got hooked. His parents were hardworking middle-class folks. His mother was a teacher and his father was a plumber.

Jim's journey progressed from partying to self-destructive drinking and drugging. He soon began dealing drugs to be able to afford his habit. His addictions pulled him down into the bowels of society.

Following a predictable self-sabotaging addict's path, he never attended college, although he is very intelligent. Instead, he settled for low-paying menial factory and construction work that allowed him to indulge in his addictions. Like many of us, he was able to find a wife, or codependent, who gave him a flimsy reed of stability in an otherwise unstable existence. I have noticed time and again the phenomenon of alcoholics and addicts attracting an outstanding significant other who tries to help save us from ourselves.

Through his thirties, Jim continued to hit new lows. The birth of a son and pleading from family members had little effect on him. Things got so bad that he resorted to self-mutilation in order to get doctors to write prescriptions for painkillers for him. He broke his own fingers, had many of his teeth pulled, and even went so far as to have his own appendix removed by pretending to have appendicitis. When he started running out of body parts and was no longer able to hold down the most menial job, Jim resorted to robbing houses. Eventually, he was caught and brought before a judge.

Jim recounted to me how that day, standing before the judge, was an enlightening experience. The judge told Jim he was a cancer. People like him were the reason our country was in decline. He was the reason people had to lock their doors. The judge held nothing back. Jim said the shock was that he never saw himself the way the judge was describing him. Self-justification, addictions, and delusions had convinced him that he was a great guy who just drank and drugged too much.

He turned and saw his parents, wife, and friends sitting in the court as the judge chastised him. He saw the look of pain in their eyes. Then it hit him. Everything the judge said was 100 percent true. He thought, *How did I get here? What happened to me?*

Jim was sentenced to nine years in the state penitentiary, which frightened and sickened him. He felt an overwhelming sense of remorse when he realized the shame his family must feel upon reading his name in the local newspaper associated with such crimes.

It looked like it was all over for Jim, but thanks to a wise judge with foresight, along with what can only be considered a gift from God, Jim was about to be saved.

The judge gave him an opportunity to change his life. He was enrolled in a strict drug rehabilitation program. He was required to attend court-mandated drug counseling. He was required to attend a twelve-step program. He was required to appear before the same judge every Monday morning for the next four years. He was required to give a urine sample three times per week for the next four years. He was required to pay for his treatment, to pay his fines, and to make restitution for his crimes. If any single commitment to which he agreed was not kept, Jim would serve out his entire prison sentence.

It would have been easy for the judge to simply incarcerate Jim for nine years and call the next case, but the wisdom of the judge has paid dividends for all concerned.

I first met Jim standing outside a sober function I was

attending. He was angry, defiant, and manipulative. But none of that mattered. What did matter was that he was in attendance.

The saying "bring the body and the mind will follow" holds true, because that's exactly what happened. Jim was exposed to a group of people with whom he could connect. People who had experienced many of the same challenges he was currently facing. He began to distance himself from his old druggie friends and began associating with sober people. Little by little, he started to change. It didn't happen overnight, but it did happen.

Over time, he grew physically stronger and his mind started to clear. Out of this newfound awareness grew a sense of possibility.

Jim's last job prior to his arrest was as a house painter. He needed money and realized he was good at painting, so he decided to go into business for himself. He could have easily focused on all the reasons he would not be successful, such as his lack of business experience or his bad reputation, but Jim chose the road less traveled. He made it his goal to deliver the best services he was capable of and priced his jobs fairly. Soon, people started hearing about this great painter and referrals started rolling in. Jim's ability to provide service for others, rather than take from others, was starting to pay off.

In a relatively short period of time, he was so busy he needed to hire more workers to help him. As his business expanded, so did his services. He was no longer a painter. He was the owner of a full-service construction company.

How did this happen? I'll tell you. He turned his power of focus from drugs and alcohol to business. As his wife puts it, "He is using his evil powers for good." Jim has lived up to his commitments and striven to keep his moral and ethical standards at the highest level. He has hired many people who are in recovery and are also proving to be excellent employees, and his company's reputation continues to grow.

> He turned his power of focus from drugs and alcohol to business. As his wife puts it, "He is using his evil powers for good."

Jim has long since completed all his court commitments. I often think back and wonder what would have happened if he hadn't encountered such a wise judge. He likely would have been sentenced, incarcerated, and become another drag on society. Instead, his wife and son have a husband and father of whom they are proud. His business is an asset to his customers and his community. He pays taxes instead of costing the taxpayer. He has grown into an outstanding entrepreneur. He is a fine example of the power of recovery.

As you'll recall, I began this chapter with the definition of the word *inspired*. Inspiration is all about spiritual, divine, supernatural influences that get communicated to an individual and the effects that they have on that person—like Jim—and others. Beyond common sense, beyond the savings in dollars, beyond all the waste and human misery, what would Jesus do? What would you do? God didn't create any human garbage and doesn't expect his children to be treated as such. If God is the father, then we are truly all brothers and sisters. Instead of pushing fear and punishment, we need to start spreading hope. To give the gift of hope to someone struggling, poor, or downtrodden is a feeling unlike any other you will ever know. You receive more than the person you are helping. It's true abundance. It's doing God's will. It's great to say you believe in God, or that you are a Christian, but the proof is in the action.

Many people today base their political affiliations on whether they are for or against abortion. Don't just protest or spend endless hours in debate about that issue; try helping someone who is pregnant or unwed. Adopt an unwanted child. Contribute to an orphanage or, better yet, spend your time and money on education to prevent unwanted pregnancies. Be a big brother or sister. Mentor someone. You get the idea. Walk the talk. Inspire others. Remember, you will receive more than the person you're trying to help.

Pray to God for solutions to our societal ills . . . creative solutions. It takes no imagination to lock someone up. It might feel good for a few minutes, but it doesn't solve the real problem. The real problem began years earlier with anxiety and lack of self-esteem.

Our country needs men and women with creative forward-thinking solutions to our common challenges. Pray for guidance. Ask the Creator where you can contribute and in what capacity. When your prayer is answered, take action. Challenge your beliefs. Don't justify or dismiss these ideas because they are new or uncomfortable.

Try starting a new habit. For example, if you are envious or resentful toward a particular person, try praying for that person for twenty-eight days (the time it takes to break an old habit). Pray for their unlimited happiness and peace of mind. Wish for them all the good things you wish for yourself. At the end of the twenty-eight days, that person might not have changed, but I guarantee you will feel better. Try it. It works!

Now, you might balk at this suggestion, and you might have a thousand good reasons as to why you have a right to be upset with this person. This type of attitude is like an infectious disease that creeps into your consciousness and exerts a baneful influence on your soul. To use myself as an example, I am a recovering alcoholic, and alcohol is poison to me. It makes no difference if I drink poison to celebrate a good time or to relieve my stress or depression; either way, if I drink poison it kills me. So it is with resentment. Whether you hold on to resentment for what you consider a justified reason or an unjustified reason, it's poison to your soul nonetheless.

Realize that you are not a human being searching for a spiritual connection; you are pure spirit having a human experience. Understanding and accepting this concept is paramount to unlocking your potential from the prison your ego has created.

Search beyond what your senses are able to perceive. Your senses often trick you into believing that the material world you inhabit is real. The eye believes what it sees. The world you perceive is as real as a shadow. Science has proven that all physical matter is made of atoms. Pure energy, intelligently organized, that gives all we see form and functionality. At a quantum level this bundle of energy is composed of 99.99999 percent empty space. All our modern technology is based on these laws. That's right: you, me, and everything we perceive as matter are really nothing more than empty space and intelligently organized energy.

How else does a computer chip the size of a postage stamp do millions of calculations simultaneously? When you look at a computer chip, it looks as plain as a piece of plastic or as nondescript as a rock, yet through our understanding of how quantum physics works, that chip is energy and intelligence in action. It is human beings, through their understanding of scientific laws, who build the potential into the chip.

When I speak of God, or the Creator, I mean the source of all that exists . . . the Creator of all potential. In many ways, this concept is too difficult for our human minds to grasp. As humans we give everything a name, which helps us understand it by restricting its function. We are always deleting and rejecting thoughts to keep everything in its proper box. I am a man so that means I am not a woman or a horse or a dog. I am an alcoholic, a father, and a writer. All these distinctions put labels and restrictions on what I believe about myself and what the world believes about me.

God is limitless, timeless, without boundaries, all power, all things. Having this human experience and human mind, we feel the need to put restrictions on our concept of God.

For example, some people believe God to be a white-haired old man with a long beard, sitting on a throne in the clouds. He spends his time writing down in his big book all the good and bad things you have ever done. Upon your demise, he either sends you to everlasting happiness or unending despair, depending on your earthly deeds.

This concept, as I understand it, makes God in the image of man rather than man in the image of God. It is an ego trip like few others. It limits God to the actions of a petty king or dictator with all the ego-centric character flaws of man.

How, then, can a concept of God be developed? I choose to look at God in the traits that I witness and attribute to God. God is life and creation, not just living, but all life and creation that ever was and ever will be. God is all abundance, joy, and growth. Our universe is expanding. Every atom that exists is expanding. Everything, even the empty space between your fingers, is expanding, and this has been scientifically proven.

When you feel happiness, you expand, you stand taller, your

physical expressions get larger; you smile and your mouth gets broader. On the other hand, when you feel fear or depression, you contract, your shoulders droop, your mouth and lips purse, your face and brow wrinkle and shrink. Our universe is expanding. Our knowledge is expanding. You are made to expand. There is no doubt in God's actions. Our God is one of joy and growth.

God is love, for without love we would not be sharing this experience. To be selfless, caring, and loving is human. It separates us from all other creatures. To love our neighbor as we love ourselves allows us the privilege of being called children of God. To love God is to be loved.

God is creative intelligence. It is humanity's privilege to be self-aware, to pursue creative intelligence in an attempt to understand the world we inhabit, and to be able to communicate this experience to our fellow humans.

God is truth and understanding. Realizing that the Creator has expressed himself through you is to be relieved of the burden of fear and doubt your ego embraces. You would not be here having the potential you have if it were not the Creator's wish.

Realizing that the Creator has expressed himself through you is to be relieved of the burden of fear and doubt your ego embraces.

God is Spirit; therefore, you and I are Spirit also. The material world is finite; the spiritual world is without end. God is the truth behind all the mathematical formulas and the constantly changing forces of nature. God is true reality and is forever manifesting and recreating itself.

These are a few of the characteristics I attribute to God. These labels I choose and the depth of my understanding limit my concept of God. Still, it is a start.

The miracle of sobriety has allowed me to expand my concept of God. This understanding has relieved much anxiety, allowing a free flow of ideas, which in turn manifest in my life as abundance.

How big is your God?

To enjoy a full recovery requires inspiration. You have to be willing to follow your dreams even if it means risking disappointment. By tapping into a power greater than yourself, you will be able to overcome the fear that ties you to mediocrity.

Nonconformity is an asset when used constructively and not selfishly. That character trait was given to you for a higher purpose. Start using it to improve not only your life but also the lives of your fellow human beings.

Let's Review

- Conformity kills. Believe in limitless possibility. Place trust in your higher power and follow your dreams.
- Divine influence and the ability to receive the sacred is the definition of inspiration. Turn on your receiver.
- Contribute to the success of others and you will be rewarded with success.
- Addiction is a symptom of a far deeper soul sickness.
- Try selling hope, not hate.

- What society considers acceptable should be challenged. Prison and punishment don't solve the root problem. When the sentence is completed the problem still exists.
- Challenge yourself. Challenge your predetermined ideas of right and wrong, success and failure, as well as what you are capable of achieving. Open your mind to the creative wisdom of the universe.

FULL RECOVERY ACTION PLAN EXERCISES

Take out your Full Recovery Action Plan. It's time to dream big dreams.

This chapter began with the observation that many people surrender their dreams and live like the walking dead. Get inspired, now, to figure out what your dreams are. Dare to dream big. Don't worry about how you will accomplish your task; just make them large enough to be inspirational. Let your mind soar with a sense of possibility.

1. What would you attempt if success were guaranteed?
2. What would you like to do with the rest of your life if you had unlimited time, freedom, and wealth? How would you contribute to the betterment of mankind?
3. How big is your God? Is your God a God of miracles? Is your God a God of love? What characteristics do you attribute to your higher power? Jesus said, "If ye being evil know how to give good gifts unto your children, how

> much more shall your Father which is in heaven give good things to them that ask?"

Follow your dreams; let go absolutely and pray for guidance.

Live Your Truth

Already I had learned from thee that because a thing is eloquently expressed it should not be as necessarily true; nor because it is uttered with stammering lips should it be supposed as false. Nor, again, is it necessarily true because badly uttered nor false because magnificently spoken.

—SAINT AUGUSTINE

LIVE YOUR TRUTH. Speak your truth. Keep your word. Sounds like a tall order, doesn't it? And it is a tall order. Up to this point, I've mainly covered techniques for moving beyond your past by adopting a new set of principles and taking action. Your memories of the past are simply a subjective, ego-based view of reality. In your memories, your ego always makes sure you are the star of the show. What I mean by this is no matter what scenario your memories project, your ego equates only with how the situation impacts you. It makes no difference if the situation is good or bad because actual reality is of no concern to the ego. Often we cling to memories because we falsely believe they define who we are. By letting go of the past you can live your truth. Misguided beliefs lead to poor results. Truth is its own reward.

Sobriety teaches us the importance of truth. Now it's time to learn how to live your truth and use the power of truth to bring you a full recovery.

Your Words Are Powerful

There is enormous power in your words. The ability to speak, write, and communicate effectively with one another is a gift from the Creator. And that ability to communicate through language is what has allowed us to shape our world. The Gospel of John says about the creation, "In the beginning was the Word, and the Word was with God, and the Word was God." That sums it up. God has given us the Word. All creation began with the Word; even ancient man recognized this truth.

Speaking and writing has allowed us to share our ideas with one another. This creative process turns thoughts into things. Words written or spoken have the ability to turn abstract thought into material form. Thought is merely intent, speaking is conveyance of that intent. Often the conveyance of intent is all that is needed to produce action.

The ability to communicate our ideas not only allows us to create but also allows others to participate in the creative process. This is why mankind is constantly advancing. Each person has the ability to use and improve on the ideas and creations of all that have gone before them. Without language this process would be impossible.

Isn't this the foundation of our educational system? We all learn the basics: reading, writing, and arithmetic. This process exposes us to the universal ideas of how to communicate effectively with one another. It also inspires us, allowing us to improve on the ideas and inventions of the past.

Our ability to speak, learn, and share ideas allows us to use the creative intelligence of others to solve predetermined problems. This saves us time and energy. Have you ever worked with a group or team to solve a problem? Just sat in a room and bounced ideas off each other? It's an amazing exercise. The more people who are consciously working to solve a problem, the more ideas get generated. New ideas give birth to even more new ideas. People seem to feed off the creativity of others. Our capitalist economic system is based on groups of people developing better strategies to serve mankind and subsequently being rewarded with money for their efforts. None of this would be possible without the ability to communicate effectively.

Here is where the challenge arises. The problem is not so much that we can't communicate effectively. The problem, quite often, is in what we choose to communicate.

> The problem is not so much that we can't communicate effectively. The problem, quite often, is in what we choose to communicate.

Many people today communicate fear. This is especially true of people in power. Parents, educators, politicians, and the media willingly participate in this activity. As I explained in detail in the chapter titled "Fear," it is a base emotion that is very powerful. When otherwise intelligent people are exposed repeatedly to negative, fearful propaganda from their leaders, many of them embrace the idea being propagated. The herd mentality takes over and the attitude people adopt is "everyone is saying it so it must be true." Consciously or unconsciously, they surrender the right to choose. Albert Einstein said it best: "A blind obedience to authority is the greatest enemy of truth."

Fearmongering has been a tool of the powerful to keep the masses under control for as far back as we are able to track. Whether it's the religious community threatening you with eternal damnation for not obeying the rules it dictates, or the government taking away your personal freedoms in the name of patriotism and security from terrorism, fear is used as a cheap and powerful commodity.

Hitler is quoted as saying, "How fortunate it is for governments that men don't think." Joseph Goebbels, Hitler's propaganda minister, said, "Make the lie big, make it simple, keep saying it, and eventually they will believe it." Hitler did not invent this. The same tactics have been repeated throughout history. Hitler simply understood human nature.

Words are so powerful they can bring worldwide calamity, as evidenced in Hitler's Nazi Germany. Words can also inspire and lead us to a higher consciousness as Franklin D. Roosevelt did when he told Americans, "The only thing we have to fear is fear itself."

To live an exciting, joyous, and successful life, you must learn to use your words intelligently. How else will you be able to attract the people and circumstances you need to fulfill your destiny? Gossip and

To live an exciting, joyous, and successful life, use your words intelligently. How else will you be able to attract the people and circumstances you need to fulfill your destiny?

the promotion of fear are the misuse of your creative energy. When you gossip or speak ill of another, it's like releasing an airborne toxin that gets inhaled by all who come in contact with its poison.

As a society, we devote untold wasted hours to this morbid pastime. Gossip shows, magazines, and newspapers are some of the most popular and profitable ventures in media today. We know more about the misadventures of Kim Kardashian than we know about our own economy and, in some cases, our own careers. We are becoming a society of voyeurs and gossipers. The end result is that whatever thoughts you consistently hold, or you focus on with emotion, you will become. You attract many of the same negative qualities into your own life that you watch and read about.

Words not only tell a story through knowledge of the topic; they also create intention. Half-truths and omissions have been raised to an art form meant to confuse intentions. It's a national disgrace that when asked, most adults believe their political leaders to be crooked or immoral. We have become so jaded that we not only accept scandal and underhandedness from our leaders, we actually expect it.

Here is where the Serenity Prayer can be put into action. I'm referring to the part that states, "the courage to change the things I can." Start today by raising your standards. Remember that by choice and repetition, habits and beliefs can be changed for good or bad. Have the *courage to change the things you can.*

Stop spreading poison. Refuse to gossip, especially in front of children. Let's break the cycle of fear and negativity. Don't accept fearmongering, immorality, and half-truths from your political leaders or the media.

Today you can live the truth . . . your truth. Realize that you are an example to all with whom you come into contact. What type of example do you want to be? How about being an example of what one recovering person can accomplish. You receive what you give. If you give gossip, half-truths, and sickness to others, that is what you will attract into your life. If you spread hope, truth, and joy to all you encounter, that is what you will attract into your life. It's yours for the choosing.

Make sure you don't misuse your words on yourself. You are speaking to yourself through your thoughts all day long. Your mind is constantly anchoring itself to a predetermined vision of what the ego tells your subconscious you are. It's estimated that up to 90 percent of all the thoughts that enter your mind on a daily basis are the exact same ones you had yesterday. Unless you make a decision to change your focus, they will be the same thoughts you will have tomorrow. If you hold negative, weak thoughts 90 percent of the time, day after day, it is very difficult to function.

Practice telling yourself statements like these:

I am living a full recovery.

I am blessed.

I am capable of creating the life I desire.

I am mentally and physically healthy.

I am a miracle.

I am successful.

I am loved.

I am wealthy.

This might be difficult at first, especially if you have a habit of thinking negatively. Keep practicing. It does get easier.

Bob's Journey to Full Recovery

I am privileged to know a man named Bob who practiced changing his internal communication and realized the truth behind his potential. Bob was raised in a dysfunctional family where addiction and anger were a normal fact of life. His childhood home was about ten minutes outside Manhattan in a working-class neighborhood in New Jersey. Bob's home just happened to be located next to a church, which he quickly learned to dislike. He has told me that he always felt that the priests and parishioners were looking down on him and his family. "If God was in the church, he never came next door to help me."

By age ten, Bob discovered alcohol and drugs. It didn't take long for him to develop a habit. Alcohol and drugs quickly became his preferred method of dealing with life's challenges. Deeply rooted self-esteem, anger, and other untreated psychological issues brought Bob's high school career to an abrupt end. He dropped out of school and became a Deadhead. He found the bohemian lifestyle following The Grateful Dead, as well as the unending party, helped him to forget the pain of his childhood. Through a poor inner dialogue Bob had convinced himself that escape via intoxication was better than conforming to the "normal," and what he perceived as hypocritical, lifestyle that he had witnessed in his hometown.

By the time Bob was in his thirties, his poor inner dialogue caught up with him. He had spent more than twenty years reinforcing a pattern of behavior that didn't work. He was now a crackhead, and the days of The Grateful Dead were long gone. He had married a girl along the way and now had a family, but his disease was shifting into overdrive. He wanted to change but didn't have a clue how. The negative thinking patterns that were anchored into his subconscious had become his reality.

Bob had convinced himself that he could not be hurt and would never get caught. He placed himself in increasingly dangerous situations. The few times he was arrested he received a relatively light punishment. This only reinforced his delusional thinking. Eventually, he committed a crime that he was held accountable for and was sentenced to prison.

Due to the nature of his offense, Bob was required to attend psychological counseling. It didn't take long for the social worker to diagnose Bob's substance abuse problem or to recognize that he was extremely intelligent. The counselor mandated alcohol and drug treatment, and Bob had to conform if he had any hope of early parole.

Bob explained to me that as he learned about the disease of addiction, he recognized that he had all the symptoms. He also learned of the spiritual approach to recovery. He decided, however, that by self-awareness alone he would be able to lick his addiction. He decided that armed with this newfound knowledge he would never need to get high again, but when it came to God and spirituality, he would have none of it. The internal conversation that he had been reinforcing since childhood kept him from seeking a higher truth.

He confided in me how he actually felt bad for the other prisoners who constantly talked about getting high because they were not as enlightened as he was. It gave him an air of superiority that he truly enjoyed. Eventually, Bob was paroled. What happened next surprised even Bob.

His wife picked him up, they hugged, and they walked to the car. The first words he spoke were, "I can really go for a burger and a beer." He wasn't even out of jail for sixty seconds and he had already forgotten the pain and humiliation that he had been experiencing while incarcerated. He told me that he completely forgot the self-awareness and feeling of superiority that had comforted him before he was released. Luckily, his wife intervened by reminding him that he would be in violation of his parole if he drank any alcohol, and sanity returned.

Following that close call, Bob decided to do whatever was necessary to stay sober, even if it meant investigating a spiritual way of life. He entered a program of recovery and stayed sober, but that is not the end of the story. The ability to improve his life by staying sober and developing a working spirituality was the enlightenment that he was seeking.

Bob has embraced the principles in this book and has reaped the rewards. Bob opened his mind and learned to reprogram his habitual ways of thinking. He has documented his fears and has found people who knew how to help him overcome them. He has recognized the truth about his own potential by searching out a God of his understanding. He has learned to communicate with himself in a more positive way through choice and repetition. He makes the most of his gifts and talents and continues to press forward.

Bob has been out of prison for eleven years and has had many challenges. He is still on parole, and the system has made it very difficult for him at times, but he lets nothing stop him. Bob did the work and has reaped the benefits. He found out what his wants and needs really are. He lives with an attitude of gratitude and his abundance grows. His relationship with his spouse has not always been easy, but they have committed themselves to the relationship, and their love endures. Bob's children are National Honor Society members and are scholastic overachievers. He built a successful business from scratch, because he chose to, that continues to thrive even in tough economic times. He owns a beautiful farm as well as investment properties and is a respected member of the business community. The truth is that Bob is the same man, with the same talents and the same potential, as the crack-smoking Deadhead. The only difference is Bob got sober and gained the courage, by developing his relationship with God, to change his inner dialogue and live the truth. He is an example of what a life of contribution, courage, and truth can accomplish. What is your truth?

I would like to end this chapter by suggesting you practice one more way of living the truth and promoting a healthy inner dialogue, which will increase your sense of peace. Don't gossip about yourself. I make it a practice not to tell my problems or misfortunes to anyone who can't help me fix them. That would be gossiping about myself. Instead, I pray for a solution and take the appropriate action needed to solve my problem.

When someone in my company gossips or tries to spread poison, I let them know I am not interested in that topic. I am not judgmental or critical; I pray for them and let it go. The sickness is within them, and they must deal with it.

The same holds true when someone gossips or spreads rumors about me. I give them no power in my life and pay them as little attention as possible. I remember that I cannot control another's thinking, only my own. It is a complete waste of time to try and play the role of gossip police. Remember the law of substitution? When the poison of gossip drifts your way, rather than focusing on a perceived wrong done to you or another, try substituting a different, more empowering thought. This is a learned skill that gets easier with practice.

I choose to focus on all the things for which I'm grateful. Another's opinion of me does not affect God's grace in my life.

The next time you're tempted to gossip behind someone's back, try a new approach. Question your motives. Ask yourself, if that person were here, would I be willing to have the same conversation? If the answer is no, then you should not be having it. If the answer is yes, consider this rhyme: Say what you mean, and mean what you say, but don't say it mean.

Remember, silence is golden and duct tape is silver.

Let's Review

- Live your truth, speak your truth, keep your word.
- Misguided ideas lead to poor results.
- Words, written or spoken, have the ability to turn abstract thoughts into material results.
- Intelligently choose what you communicate to the world and to yourself.
- Truth is its own reward. Substitute gratitude for fear.
- Promotion of gossip and fear are the misuse of the word.

FULL RECOVERY ACTION PLAN EXERCISES

Take out your Full Recovery Action Plan. Do you misuse your words on yourself or on others? Try this exercise.

For a period of one day, write down every time you gossip about anyone. Also include any time you think negative or defeatist thoughts about yourself or anyone else. You might be surprised at the results.

Now, make a list of five empowering or grateful suggestions you can substitute in your consciousness the next time you catch yourself drifting.

PART III

DEDICATION

GPS: Goals Produce Success

Great things are not done by impulse, but by a series of small things brought together.
—VINCENT VAN GOGH

MANY NEW AUTOMOBILES today are equipped with a GPS navigation system. The GPS, or Global Positioning System, tracks the movement of the vehicle and gives explicit directions that make it virtually impossible to get lost. The driver is supplied with a road map and directions to ensure that he arrives at his destination as efficiently as possible and in the shortest amount of time.

Today, you are about to develop your own road map to success. The letters "GPS" in your personal system, however, stand for Goals Produce Success. This GPS system will be the process that will guide you as efficiently as possible to your ultimate destination—a full recovery.

"Life begins at the level of action." That is a quote from a wise friend of mine, Farmer Bill. What I have been encouraging you to do from the first chapter in this book is to take action. You started by getting to know yourself, your strengths, weaknesses, fears, desires, and beliefs. You have been given the tools to ask better questions, lift the veil of the ego, and challenge the status quo. Now that you have some insight as to what makes you tick, you should be spiritually grounded enough to make better choices concerning your ability to reach your potential. It's time to continue the journey by drawing up a road map to success. Writing down your goals is an action step. Your goals are your destination.

Setting Your Goals

If you don't know where you're going, any road will get you there. You can choose right now which direction you want to go. All people daydream about what they want to do, own, or accomplish in life. That's the easy part. What's amazing is the lack of enthusiasm I've observed among men and women when it comes to taking action to turn their dreams into reality.

You may have heard of a famous study done at Yale University in 1953. Members of the graduating class were interviewed regarding their future plans and what they hoped to accomplish. There were many noteworthy responses considering the level of talent and educational achievements of the graduates. After listening to the responses, the interviewers asked the students how many had written down their goals and had a plan of action to accomplish them. Only 3 percent of the students had written down their goals, so that left 97 percent with good intentions.

At the twenty-year reunion of the Class of 1953, the interviewers sat down for a second interview with the surviving class members. They documented that the people who had clear written goals, which were reviewed and updated regularly, seemed to be the happiest and most successful of their class.

That was all fine and good, but happiness is very subjective and difficult to measure. What was measurable, though, was that the 3 percent of the graduates who had written goals had a monetary worth in excess of the 97 percent who did not write down their goals. That's right: the 3 percent were worth more than the other 97 percent combined. Now that's what I call measurable!

When it comes to goals, the faintest ink is better than the sharpest memory. Goals need to be written. GPS: Goals Produce Success. This holds true for the smallest to the largest goals.

Have you ever gotten out of bed in the morning and thought about what you wanted to accomplish that day and then, having gone through the day, realized you hadn't accomplished anything you wanted? Sure you were busy. There were phones to answer, bills to pay, conversations to be had, dishes to wash, but at the end of the day you were no further along in your quest of fulfilling your dreams than when you woke up.

When it comes to goals, the faintest ink is better than the sharpest memory.

Another example is shopping. I'll set the scene. You look in the refrigerator and decide you need a few items. You make a mental note and proceed to the grocery store. You arrive home a short time later with items you didn't actually need and forgot to purchase some of the items that prompted you to go shopping in the first place.

Take the same scenario, except this time, write a list of what you want to purchase at the store. Ninety-nine percent of the time you come home with all the items on your list and not a lot of things you really don't need. Writing a shopping list is no more than setting a mini-goal. GPS: Goals Produce Success. Goals give you direction as well as a measurable outcome for your efforts.

I have a simple suggestion that I guarantee will help you to become more successful. At some point every day, take a few minutes and write down exactly what you want to accomplish in the next twenty-four hours. I like to do it in the evening, and then I review and edit my list first thing in the morning.

Next, rank all of the items on your list in order of importance. If there are ten items you want to accomplish, number one should be the most important and number ten the least important. When you begin your day, take out your list and start with number one, the most important task you need to accomplish that day. Finish it completely before you move on to number two, number three, and so on. At the end of the day, look at your list and see if any items haven't been crossed off. If you feel they are still important, put them on the next day's list.

This simple idea of writing a to-do list on a daily basis can give you a road map for planning your day's events. Make sure you number your tasks in order of importance so that if you don't complete them all, you at least get the most pressing items done. When someone or something throws you a curveball, or you hit a bump in the road, look at your list and get back on track. This simple program of daily goals helps you stay focused and keeps you from getting sidetracked.

In addition to writing daily goals, it is imperative that you develop a habit of being able to nicely say no to people who try to waste your time. When you find someone or something grabbing for your attention that doesn't fit in with your primary goal for the day, reviewing your list will bring you back on course. Developing this simple habit pays untold dividends and will increase your productivity.

I used to fall into the one-minute trap. "Brian, you got a minute?" was what I heard all day long. The problem is that nothing ever takes a minute. Many of the questions and problems people wanted me to solve or get involved with were not important to me or my goals. I learned to tactfully say no. I learned to set aside blocks of fifteen minutes to one hour of time a few times a week when I would be available to answer questions. *One-minute* questions, that is.

I also developed the habit of not entertaining questions or dealing with problems that people can solve on their own. If you are a leader, manager, parent, or teacher, it's better to teach people to think for themselves. The idea is to encourage them to come up with the answers and be able to explain the process if necessary. It doesn't do you or the other person any good for you to think for him or her. Sure, mistakes will be made and you must be a little patient. However, in the long run, you'll find you have more time to attend to your priorities if you teach others to think on their own.

The Creator endowed us all with a thinking apparatus known as the brain. Your brain, much like a muscle, will atrophy if it's not exercised. I have personal experience in both these areas. My muscles atrophied during a long hospital stay and worse yet, my brain atrophied after years of alcohol and drug abuse. Luckily, we humans are very resilient.

You may find yourself in a similar situation. Maybe you are trying to break an addiction and struggling. Perhaps you are managing your addictive personality but are still not able to demonstrate success in other areas of your life. I would like to show you the power of goal setting by sharing part of my experience, along with the actions I took and the results I achieved.

Brian's Journey to Full Recovery

After twenty years of drinking and drugging, I landed in rehab. When I left that twenty-eight-day program, I was acutely aware of a few things. The first was that my life was a mess. I was deeply in debt and could barely think. The second was that if I didn't stay sober I had no future. I probably would be better off dead. I didn't believe I had another chance left.

The twenty-eight days I put together without a drink or a drug amazed me. I was told that anything I put before my sobriety I would lose anyway, so I'd better put my recovery first.

I started attending a program of recovery the day I left rehab. When I was in a meeting I had no desire to get high, but when I left the meeting, my thoughts would wander and the old negative tapes in my mind would begin to play. I soon came to the conclusion that if I did not stay busy and keep my mind occupied, it would only be a matter of time before I picked up again. I remember hearing my grandmother tell me during my childhood that an idle mind is the devil's workshop, and in my case this was true. I needed to stay out of my own head.

I was able to land a menial job, but I soon realized that I could not afford to pay my bills, never mind pay back debts or save for the future. I was forced to work a second full-time job to make ends meet. It was grueling. I was at work, at a meeting, or at home trying to save my marriage. Soon it became apparent that I could not keep up that pace forever. My desperate situation forced me to seek alternative solutions. I had come to the conclusion that by following suggestions from sober people, I was staying sober, too. I began to wonder, then, whether the same process would work in other areas of my life, such as finances.

This was a big leap for me. For years I used my addiction, lack of education, and other excuses as reasons that I had not become financially successful up until that point. These excuses had become so ingrained into the core of my personality that I didn't even realize I had accepted them as truth.

Now that I was trying to the best of my ability to live an honest life, I would have to cast these excuses aside and be willing to live up to my potential. I asked my higher power to guide me and began my quest.

I started right where I was. I began speaking to people I met in recovery who seemed to be happy and financially secure. There is a saying, "Take what you need and leave the rest," and that's exactly what I did. I would humble myself, ask questions, and listen intently to the answers. I did not take all the advice I was given, always remembering that advice is the cheapest commodity on the planet and worth everything it costs. Still, it was important for me to get in the habit of asking questions and to accept the fact that I didn't have all the answers. I also developed the habit of not reacting but instead thinking things through and weighing the advice I was given.

During this early phase of my recovery, I met a man named Tom who gave me advice that would change my life. He told me that some of my biggest character defects could actually be my greatest assets; I just had to be willing to put them to good use. At first I didn't understand what he meant and asked him to explain. He said that we are all endowed with gifts from the

Creator, and what we do with these gifts largely defines our ability to be happy and productive.

He continued with an observation about my ability to read people, to handle stress, and to be a survivor. These qualities were part of my gifts. He went on to explain that the same qualities that kept me alive as an active alcoholic and addict were all essential qualities to possess in the business world. "These qualities aren't taught in Harvard Business School; either you have them or you don't." Finally, Tom told me that if I could focus my energies, make good use of my gifts, and combine them with the moral standards associated with recovery, I would be an unstoppable force in business.

> Some of my biggest character defects could actually be my greatest assets; I just had to be willing to put them to good use.

I pondered our conversation and prayed over it. I became convinced that I had been wasting my talents and decided to put them to good use. I began reading all I could about success and successful people. One thing kept coming through loud and clear: all successful people have goals, and all mega-successful people write them down. This might not be new to you, but as I mentioned previously, life begins at the level of action. I had tried writing my goals down years earlier, but my lack of direction, lack of follow-through, and . . . oh yeah, drunkenness, kept me from achieving anything noteworthy. Now, even though I was still in early sobriety and not sure which direction to head, I refused to let that stop me. I decided that I did have the ability to take action and I would see where that action would lead.

When it came time to put my goals in writing, I started to hesitate. Doubt began to creep in. Was I asking too much? Isn't being sober enough? Can I really accomplish my goals?

Then I thought back to my conversation with Tom. How some of my biggest character defects could be some of my greatest assets if used constructively. I thought about the most basic character defect I had as an alcoholic/addict: to put it simply, I was addicted to "more." I wanted more of everything. Too much was never enough. I decided to use this character defect to help me move forward.

I wrote a lot of goals with regard to spirituality, family, and finances. *Big goals!* Goals I had no idea how to accomplish, but I knew if I could muster enough faith, I would reach them. This faith developed from my ability not to drink and drug one day at a time. For years I had considered it impossible to get sober, yet here I was.

Rather than running from my defects, I started to understand that there are no coincidences. Everything the Creator built into me can be put to good use. The question is, used for what purpose? Used to help what group or individual? I hear people ask, "Why is this happening to me?" when some perceived calamity comes along. Maybe it's just so you could tell the next person how to get through it.

During this period of my life, I was working for a national retailer unloading trucks, down-stocking shelves, and helping customers. My first written goal was, "I will live in recovery one day at a time." The next one I wrote was, "I will be a millionaire." Keep in mind that at that point in time I was earning less than ten dollars per hour. The next goal I wrote was, "I will be the store manager."

I described my future accomplishments in detail. I gave myself a deadline. This is very important. You want to have a definite timeline as to when you will arrive at your destination. When you take a trip on an airplane, for example, you know the place and time of your departure, where you are going to arrive, and at what time you are going to get there. The same process can be used on your journey to success. Giving yourself an exact time for when you will achieve your goals keeps leverage on you to stay focused.

I wrote all kinds of goals. I wrote that I was going to build the house of my dreams and described it in detail. I wrote about the type of husband and father I would be. I wrote about the type of truck I wanted to own. At the time, I was driving a 1965 Ford pickup truck that I prayed daily would get me to work without breaking down. I wrote lofty goals, some short-term (less than one year), others long-term (more than five years).

I use the word *lofty* because many of them were such a stretch. An example would be the goal of becoming the store manager. I had no college degree, I had no retail experience, and I had just left rehab. The store I worked at did more than $50 million a year in sales and had two hundred-plus employees.

Every time I began to ask myself, "How am I going to accomplish these goals?" I became overwhelmed. This was not very productive. So I asked myself a different question. Instead of asking how I would accomplish my goals, I decided to concentrate on the purpose for accomplishing my goals. I began to focus on where I was going rather than on the doubt and defeat of my past.

I knew from my venture into sobriety that if I could keep my faith strong, God would guide me on my journey. I wrote down the purpose for accomplishing my goals with as much emotion and heartfelt sincerity as I could muster. These reasons for doing what I was doing were meant to inspire me.

The reasons I needed to succeed started with my wife and son. I had many amends to make for the life I had given them up until that point. My reasons were written with commitments to my family, my Creator, and myself. I used the "whys" to keep pushing me forward when the going got tough.

Another way of keeping leverage on yourself is to tell your goals to another person. When you make a commitment to the important people in your life, you will feel even more obligated to press ahead. The reasons why I must succeed left me no room for retreat. I knew if I viewed failure as an option, I would undoubtedly find ways to justify taking that option. Failure was not an option.

After I had listed *why* I was committed to success, the *how* part of accomplishing my goals became apparent. I kept it real simple: I would learn everything I could about the business by asking as many questions as possible. I would align myself with people who could help me achieve my goals. I described the type of man I would be: honest, industrious, and hardworking. I would let God guide my decisions.

The first position I set my sights on was "Lead Man." I told the Lead Man I worked under that I would devote all my time and energy to making him look good. I would work for his advancement, and in turn, I asked him to teach me what he knew about the business. I learned his position. I encouraged him to delegate as much of his work to me as possible. I also encouraged him to use his free time to learn about his supervisor's position.

Many people waste valuable time trying to undermine their boss or people in authority. I did just the opposite. Nonconforming ways of thinking, which in the past had been used as a character defect, were now used constructively and turned into an asset. I realized that the quickest way to get myself promoted and acquire my supervisor's position was to get him promoted and out of the way. This realization proved to be very valuable. Not only did I form a true working partnership with this man, I also was promoted thanks in part to his recommendations.

A nice by-product of my way of thinking was that I earned the reputation of being a team player, and this reputation quickly found its way to the ears of upper management. I kept my commitment to this man and pushed him through the management ranks. When he got promoted, I got promoted, until the time finally came when he was no longer comfortable climbing the ladder of success. I, on the other hand, decided to reach my potential.

With every promotion, I learned more about the business and was exposed to more people capable of helping me reach my goals. One time along the way, I was not promoted immediately to the next level. My position was given to an outside hire. This was a setback, but with every adversity there is a lesson to be learned. At first I was hurt and angry. I believed I had earned my promotion. My first inclination was to be bitter and let the new hire struggle. Then I remembered my goals and why I needed to accomplish them. What was the goal? The goal was to be promoted, to be the store manager, to be a millionaire! So I went right back to the plan. I trained the new hire, and within five months he was promoted into a new position.

I kept my goals in front of me and read them daily. They became my main focus in life. Within two years of writing those goals, I was the store manager. In four years, I was a corporate buyer responsible for the mid-Atlantic division. Within five years, I was the district manager. I was responsible for more than eighteen hundred employees and achieved sales in excess of $460 million a year. I received much recognition from the CEO and board members. More important, I received recognition through a larger paycheck.

How did this happen? It started by being dissatisfied with my life and making a decision to change. Next, I wrote down my goals and the reasons I was absolutely committed to accomplishing them. I kept my goals in front of me and reviewed them daily, making adjustments whenever necessary. I made a conscious effort to use the gifts that God gave me. I turned my character defects into assets and developed a working faith that would help me achieve my goals. Clear goals create inspiration. GPS: Goals Produce Success.

The reasons for setting my goals were not just to buy things, even though a by-product of success is the ability to afford nicer things. For me, things would not be enough. For me, the ability to manifest abundance in all areas of my life and share it with others drives me forward.

Goals come true when they become part of your psyche. You need emotion and leverage on yourself to push on.

Remember to have fun. If you can't have fun along the way, it's not worth it. Don't get me wrong; there will be many times of frustration and disappointment. That's the reason you need to write down why you are committed to achieving your goals.

Goals come true when they become part of your psyche. Don't quit before the miracle happens. Use your dissatisfaction and your frustration to push you toward success.

Don't quit before the miracle happens. Focus on the summit, not the rocky crevices and boulders you will encounter on your climb. Use your dissatisfaction and your frustration to push you toward success. It's much easier than letting them drag you into mediocrity.

Don't Let Fear Prevent You from Reaching Your Goals

Today is probably not the first time you've heard about the importance of setting measurable goals. Most people have, but few take the consistent action needed to accomplish them. Why is this, you might ask? The answer is fear. Baseless fears, such as people will no longer like you, or friends and family will be envious of your success. Fear of not being able to achieve your goals, so you hide behind procrastination or use some other type of approach-avoidance. This leads us back again to the reality that the brain fears pain. The brain thinks it might not be able to succeed, so it tells you it's less painful not to try rather than to try and possibly fail.

This thought process is flawed. Just because you haven't achieved massive success up to this point doesn't mean it's not waiting just around the corner. Start living with a sense of expectancy. Expect good things to happen.

I expect to succeed, so I usually do. Even if I don't get the exact result or outcome I was striving to achieve, I always learn something from the experience. Many of my plans didn't turn out as I had hoped. When I review the results, I'm able to make distinctions that have turned some of my biggest blunders into success. Recall the story I shared in an earlier chapter about the inventor of the Post-it Note. He was trying to invent glue that was permanent, but it didn't work.

The key is to get into the habit of taking action and following through. If you don't get the results you want, review the situation and take another action. It's important to be aware of the results you are achieving. There might be a "Post-it Note" in the results that lead you to a new way of life. Nothing is ever a failure until you accept it as such. The only way to really fail is to not try.

I have been blessed by being allowed to participate in the process of recovery from addiction. I refuse to live in fear. The Creator guides my steps. This is how I communicate with myself and with the world around me. Understanding and accepting this principle allows me to live with expectancy and expand beyond my own limited talents and beliefs. Don't you deserve the same peace of mind?

Sometimes it's hard to see just how far I've come because I'm too close to the action. That's when I take out copies of my old goals and review them. My old goals give me a yardstick with which to measure my progress. This progress has been made one day at a time by doing the best I can for a twenty-four-hour period, letting go of yesterday and expecting good things to happen tomorrow.

Recently, I was looking back on my goal of becoming a store manager and how big that goal was at the time. Now that my understanding and abundance awareness have changed, I would not consider that as a new goal. I never want to go backward because that would be settling for less than living my potential.

When I start getting bored or too comfortable in any area of my life, I know it's time to set larger, more inspiring goals. I have also noticed with my goals, just like in my recovery, that if I don't keep moving forward I start to slip backward.

⁂

Setting goals and succeeding in attaining them is more fun when shared with others. Look at any team sport—football, for example. Can you imagine what sheer drudgery it would be if two teams suited up, took the field, and just pounded each other for an hour with no one ever having the opportunity to score a goal? It would be pretty miserable. That's why it's important to celebrate with your teammates whenever you score a first down or a touchdown, not just winning the game. By celebrating all the little successes along the way, you keep yourself and your teammates motivated and emotionally elevated. This gives you a better chance of winning. Keep it fun.

Let's Review

- GPS: Goals Produce Success.
- Goals give you direction and without direction in your life, you are like a piece of paper blowing in the wind. You get pushed, blown, and acted upon by any stimulus put against you. This is the opposite of empowerment and forces you to live in a constant state of reaction.
- Goals are the ability to create your future now.
- Goals must be written. Writing your goals is the first action step toward their fulfillment.
- Get in the habit of writing daily goals or to-do lists. You should also have short-term goals of less than one year and long-term goals of more than five years.

- When writing goals, make sure you include spiritual, family, personal, material, and financial goals.
- It's important to give yourself as many reasons as you can imagine for needing to accomplish your task. Emotional reasons you are committed to succeed are even more important than how you will reach the goal line. Reasons create leverage.
- Associate pleasure with achieving your goals and discomfort with not trying.
- Make sure you have fun and celebrate as you see yourself advancing.
- Ask yourself, Who is already getting the result I desire? Who can help me on my journey? Enlist the help of a sponsor, teacher, or mentor.

FULL RECOVERY ACTION PLAN EXERCISES

Take out your Full Recovery Action Plan. You are now ready to create your future. Remember to think big.

Start by writing at least five goals in each of the following categories. Make sure you put a timeline on when you are committed to achieving your goal.

Spiritual
Personal
Family
Career
Financial
Other important areas

Let your mind soar. No limits.

- Do you want a yacht? Would you like to earn $100 thousand or better yet, $100 million?
- What about education? Do you regret not graduating from college? Would you like to earn a PhD?
- Are you drawn toward service work? Would you like to be a missionary or do you want to join the Peace Corps?
- Do you need to lose weight or to start exercising? Is it time to quit smoking?

The important thing is that the goals must be emotional and inspirational to you. Whatever your dreams and aspirations, write them down.

Part two is to write down at least five reasons—both positive and negative—why you must accomplish your goal. This is very important because it puts leverage on you. The emotional reasons push you forward, keeping you focused and motivated when you feel like giving up.

It would look something like this:

I ________________________________ (whatever your name is) will earn $5 million by December 15, 2021. I am committed to reaching my goal because:

- My family deserves the best life has to offer.
- My Creator gave me the talent and creativity to be an example to the world.
- I will be able to send my children to college.
- I will be an example of what recovery is all about.

- I will be able to help those less fortunate than myself.
- I will live my destiny and prove myself deserving of this gift of life.

You can write as many reasons as you want. Also put down negative reasons you must accomplish your goal. Some examples would be:

- If I don't take daily action to accomplish my goal, I will be letting down all those who stood behind me for years, such as my God, my family, my friends, and most important, myself.
- I don't want to have to rely on charity in my old age.
- I don't want to come to the end of my life and have the realization that I haven't reached my potential.
- If I don't earn enough money I won't be able to travel the world.
- I don't want anyone but me to decide what I am capable of earning during my lifetime.

Remember, we are motivated as human beings by our perceptions of pleasure and pain. The quickest way to accomplish any task is to associate lots of happiness with completing the task, and lots of discomfort or pain with not succeeding. That's why you need huge goals . . . grand goals . . . goals that inspire you to reach your full potential.

Don't forget, nothing has any meaning but the meaning you give it. Make your goals fun. When I started this process,

I convinced myself that the work was fun. I started as soon as I woke up in the morning and reaffirmed it all day long. I literally told myself *work is fun* hundreds of times a day until I believed it. This habit gave me added strength and stamina during my hectic climb up the ladder of success. Tell yourself that pressing forward is exciting and enjoyable, and it will become so.

Last, keep your goals in front of you. Put them on your computer. I put copies of my goals on my dresser. I used to write them on index cards and leave them in my truck. I kept them inside my locker at work. I made sure I read them every day until they became part of my subconscious. Whatever you focus on and think about, you will attract into your life—good or bad. Start focusing on abundance instead of lack. Health instead of sickness. Success instead of failure.

Go for it!

Your Project

Know what you want, know what makes you feel good about your Self, know what brings you into harmony with others.

—I CHING

THE FEARLESSNESS and perseverance you have shown since committing to the process of self-discovery presented in this book has brought you to this point. It's time now for another action step toward full recovery. You are ready to choose your project. Before we continue, however, let's review the steps you have taken toward reaching your full potential and manifesting abundance:

1. You have systematically gotten to know yourself by examining your strengths and weaknesses.
2. You have been taught techniques to overcome fear and doubt.
3. You understand that whatever you associate with pain or with happiness will determine which path your life will follow. If you want to change a belief or action, associate

pain with the belief that you want to change and pleasure with the new belief you wish to adopt.

4. You understand that to keep expanding and moving forward in all areas of life, you must continually ask yourself the right questions.

5. You realize that whatever you focus on with emotion will eventually materialize in your life, so you must intelligently choose the thoughts that you allow to enter your mind.

6. You understand that when you hold thoughts of gratitude, love, success, and abundance consistently, and then follow them up with action, you will receive in accordance with your faith.

7. You have learned to keep an attitude of gratitude and check your motives. This is an important habit to develop in order to avoid the dangers of self-justification and an ego-driven life.

8. You realize that you are already successful and wealthy. To whom much is given, much is expected. Live with honor, truth, loyalty, and inspiration, and be careful how you communicate with yourself and others.

9. You have been given the tools to figure out what you want, as well as how to set measurable goals to focus your energy.

So, now that you have your goals, it's time to decide which destination you'll plug into your personal GPS—Goals Produce Success—system. What is your project?

When I was preparing to write this section, I remembered a story about Alexander the Great and a "project" in which he was involved. Alexander had set his sights on conquering an island whose inhabitants had a particularly nasty reputation. Because of this, Alexander noticed that doubt seemed to be creeping into his army's ranks and they were lacking enthusiasm for the project.

Being a true leader and master motivator, Alexander knew just how to handle the challenge and get leverage on his men. When his soldiers landed on the island beach, the first order Alexander gave was to gather all the boats and burn them. Then, standing in front of the burning boats, he gave a speech that has lasted through the ages. He told his men there would be no retreat. They had burned their means of escape. Together they would all march across the land to victory and sail home in their enemy's ships.

Now that's what I call attacking a project. It goes without saying that Alexander the Great and his men were successful, and they sailed home in the conquered enemy's ships.

Writing this book has been in the back of my mind for years. It has been my project for the last thirteen months. It was part of my list of long-term goals and finally made it to the top of that list.

I have enjoyed several large projects and many smaller ones in recovery. I told you about my foray into the retail world. Since leaving that retail business, I have started, owned, and operated a maintenance business, a real estate investment business, and a construction company. This is all in addition to my number-one project of staying sober and drug-free. I am currently serving as CEO of the Full Recovery Wellness Center. The Full Recovery substance abuse program integrates cutting-edge clinical therapies with spiritual, emotional, and career counseling. I am not trying to impress you, but rather impress upon you, that with God all things are possible.

Remember that the ego hates change. It tries to keep itself alive by tricking you into identifying what you do with who you are. The two are not the same. Oftentimes friends, family, and employers try to do the same to you. They like to keep you in the role they are comfortable with.

I have been told comments such as these:

- What makes you think you can accomplish such and such?
- You are an alcoholic with no college degree. You can't be the store manager.
- You are a retail manager. You don't know construction.
- You don't know enough about real estate investment to risk that kind of money.
- You don't know how to write a book.

I didn't know how to walk or use a toilet at one time either, but with a little help, guidance, and the ability to take action, I figured it out. You did too. Don't ever let anyone convince you not to try something new or outside your comfort zone simply because you haven't done it before.

So, once again I ask you, what is your project? How big are your dreams? Do you want $100 million? Are you seeking your life's purpose? Do you want to find your soul mate or climb Mount Everest? Maybe you want to become a missionary. Where do you see yourself living and working in the next five years and beyond? Your project should be associated with your dreams and desires.

Let's assume your project has to do with your career path or your ability to manifest material abundance. Understand this simple fact: You are as entitled to all the financial security, wealth, and prosperity as anyone else who ever lived on this planet. The Creator of the universe plays no favorites. We are all loved. Jesus summed it up in his Sermon on the Mount when he said, "Ask, and it shall be given you; seek, and you shall find; knock and it shall be opened unto you. For everyone that asks receives; and he that seeks will find; and to him that knocks it shall be opened."

> Don't ever let anyone convince you not to try something new or outside your comfort zone simply because you haven't done it before.

Take Action

It is now time to take action. No matter what business or career path you choose to follow, there are certain qualities or characteristics you must demonstrate if you are going to be successful. This includes, of course, retaining a good reputation while enjoying peace of mind.

Think Big

Don't settle. I have discovered it takes no more effort to close a large deal than a small one. The process is usually the same, but the numbers have more zeros on the end. In real estate, for example, it takes the same amount of time and effort to purchase or sell a multimillion-dollar property as a two-hundred-thousand-dollar property. In fact, sometimes it takes less effort when dealing with the multimillion-dollar property because usually the buyers are in a stronger position as far as credit and income than someone at the lower economic level. Don't be afraid of big numbers. Big numbers often equate to big profits.

Insist on Excellence

For yourself, and all with whom you choose to associate, insist on excellence. Quality must always precede quantity. Offer superior service to all you encounter. You will be rewarded in direct proportion to the service you give. Poor service = poor rewards. Good service = good rewards. Great service = great rewards. Give more than you are required, and you will receive more than you expect.

Don't Fear the Word *No*

The Creator of the universe is on your team. You are here to fulfill your destiny. As an addict, you no doubt perfected the skill of ignoring the word *no,* as well as practiced the art of defiance. Whatever addiction in which you indulged, people have tried to help you by saying no, and you ignored them and did what you wanted anyway. Now is the time to draw out that character trait. God instilled that character trait in you for some greater purpose. Use it constructively for your good and the good of all mankind.

When someone or something attempts to block you from achieving your goal or completing your project, ignore them and boldly press forward. This does not mean that you are to be rude, arrogant, or condescending in any way. Always remember that humility and good manners go hand in hand with success.

Rather than focusing on the word *no* or stopping when confronted by an obstacle, choose to dream bigger dreams and focus on the person of excellence you are. Your supply doesn't come from any person or business entity. Your supply comes from within. The kingdom of God is within you. All things materially and spiritually come from the same source . . . the only source. "Acquaint now thyself with Him and be at peace: thereby good shall come unto thee." This is good advice from the book of Job.

Discipline Yourself

If you don't discipline yourself, someone else will. Take action daily to improve yourself. Set time aside every day, preferably in the morning, to work on your project. I say preferably in the morning because you are fresh and not yet burdened by the distractions that come up throughout the day. Try waking up at least one hour earlier and turning your focus immediately to increasing the quality of your chosen project and you will be amazed at the results.

Keep a Positive Attitude

A pleasing attitude is essential to achieving a successful outcome on your project. Remember, success is built one day at a time. Learn to love what you do. Build on your small victories and learn from your challenges. All life takes place in the present. Do your best today. Enjoy your plans, but live in the now.

Expect and Accept Problems

Challenges and unforeseen situations are a fact of life. You already know this to be true, so don't get too upset when they arise. Realize that you have the built-in potential to solve them.

Don't just react and or live in the problem. Stay focused on the solution. As it's written in Psalms, "Be still and know that I am God."

The best way to handle a problem is to calm yourself before taking any action. Turn it over to a power greater than yourself. Weigh your options and check your motives. When a solution presents itself, take action and don't be afraid to go against the tide. This may seem like a time-consuming process, but like all habits, it becomes quicker and almost automatic with practice.

Think Like a Customer

To think like a customer, you must know who your customer is. This is why it is so important to know your product and learn as much as possible about the end user. No matter what profession you are employed in, you have customers. Anyone who gives you money is a customer. This includes your employer if you work for someone, the taxpayers if you are in a government position, the stockholders if you are in the corporate world, the congregation if you are in the clergy. No matter what your position, you serve someone. The person to whom you give service is your customer.

Never take your customer for granted. Remember that your customer has both monetary and time constraints; respect them both. "Love your neighbor as you love yourself." Treat your customers as you would like to be treated. This also ties into my next suggestion.

Respect Your Coworkers and Employees

Realize that your success depends largely on others. Your coworkers and employees are partners in your business. Teach them to treat your customers with the same respect that you show them. Educate them to the fact that every customer who chooses to frequent your business is paying their salary. The owner is not paying the employees' salaries, the customer is. It is the customer, not the business, that puts food on their table, pays their family's bills, and provides education and health care to both you and them.

Whether you realize it or not, your associates or employees take all their cues from you. Consistency is the mark of a true leader. Do not show favoritism among your employees.

Use restraint when dealing with difficult coworkers; no one likes to be talked down to. Praise in public, correct in private. Remember the Golden Rule: "Do unto others as you would have done unto you."

Be Creative

Don't be afraid to try new things. Be yourself. Don't let the fear of failure keep you from experiencing all the joy and success you deserve. You are unique. The Creator has built into you special gifts and unlimited potential.

Ask your family, friends, associates, and coworkers for suggestions on how to improve your project. No one knows everything. This process builds a sense of belonging, appreciation, and teamwork.

Give credit where credit is due. When an associate or coworker displays an exceptional quality or comes up with a good idea, make sure to give her or him credit. Not only is it the right thing to do, it will also encourage those individuals and others to keep contributing new ideas. Stay humble.

Keep Increasing Your Knowledge

There is no substitute for education. The marketplace and the technology used in your project are constantly changing. To be a true professional now and in the future, you must keep increasing your knowledge and remain an expert in your chosen field.

Live with Enthusiasm

If you are not passionate about your project, no one else will be. It's important to choose a project that excites you.

Forget about the money for a moment. Money is just a scorecard that shows how well you serve others. Be passionate, choose a project that complements your natural abilities and interests, and you will become successful. Be successful and the money will follow. Do what you love and work becomes play. When you are no longer passionate about your project, find a bigger project.

Since getting sober, I have enjoyed several corporate positions, as well as started and operated several businesses. Some people find one project they feel passionate enough about to pursue until the day they die. I am a real type A personality whose natural curiosity pulls me in many directions. I have been extremely successful in some of my business ventures and just plain old successful with others.

Keep in mind that success and failure are self-defined. My definition of success is "deliberately pursuing a worthy goal." That means if you have chosen to work on a predetermined project by taking deliberate action toward turning it into reality, you are already a success. By this definition of success, as soon as you begin to take action, you are succeeding.

If you have chosen to work on a predetermined project by taking deliberate action toward turning it into reality, you are already a success.

Hindsight being 20/20, I've noticed that the projects that really didn't challenge me or complement my natural instincts were the ones in which I quickly lost interest. That doesn't mean I wasn't successful or that the projects weren't profitable. It simply means that when I had to force myself to stay passionate, I was ready for a new project. I consider this realization a strength rather than a weakness. When I come to the realization that I have outgrown my project, I start getting excited because I know I am about to increase my knowledge in a new environment.

If you aren't happy with yourself or your career, don't fear change, just find a new project. Life should be an exciting adventure, not a chore to be endured. Trust your gut. Make life a game you can win.

Embody Character, Ethics, and Morals

Success and money are addictive. As you know, addiction often allows you to justify misguided behavior. Many in business believe the ends justify the means. If you have to lie, cheat, steal, gossip, or ruin your competitor's reputation by any means possible, so be it. The law of the jungle is kill or be killed.

Prior to my recovery, I lived by this code. I no longer do. Judging from most of the self-help literature I have read, as well as my own experience in the corporate world, I seem to be the minority. I can only share my own experience.

I like a good business deal as much as the next person. I negotiate in complete fairness with everyone with whom I do business. I expect to be treated fairly and treat others the same way. I honestly believe in the win-win concept, though it is only possible when you're negotiating with someone willing to try it.

Most of the long-term business relationships I have developed over the past twenty years are with people who are willing to adopt this concept. Through a willingness to appreciate another's point of view, I have developed a network of business associates whose businesses and bottom-line profits keep expanding.

It is a lot of hard work, time, and effort to develop working relationships and business contacts. When I find people willing to accept the idea that we can all earn money through enlightened cooperation, it's like hitting the lottery. Our common interests allow us to grow and prosper together. Unlike the lottery, it's not just a one-time win. It's the gift that keeps on giving. By developing the relationship, we have an opportunity to win over and over again. Every time we do business or close a deal, we both get paid.

Believing in the win-win concept means we both win. I don't let anyone take advantage of me in any deal. I surround myself with people of character who keep their word and deliver a quality product. If someone is not willing to live by the win-win ethic, I avoid doing business with him or her.

Expect Your Project to Succeed

Live with expectancy. Many people suffer from the "what-if" syndrome. They live in constant fear of what might happen. A good measure of common sense is always recommended when making difficult decisions regarding your project, but many fears and worries are nothing more than misguided fantasies. A good rule of thumb for making a difficult decision or confronting a challenge is to ask yourself this question: Would I take this action if I were fearless? What's keeping you from asking for that raise? Is it fear of hearing the word *no*? If you honestly feel you have earned it, then it's time to ask for a raise. Ego-based fear of uncertainty keeps us from taking the positive actions that often result in prosperity.

Always start with the attitude that your project will succeed. If you don't believe it will succeed, why did you choose it?

Always start with the attitude that your project will succeed. If you don't believe it will succeed, why did you choose it?

When I choose a new project, I start with the unwavering belief that it will succeed. I hire and solicit input from the best people I can afford. I weigh all ideas and follow my instincts. I expect to succeed and I usually do.

I have been called lucky. I know people who resent me for it, but that's their problem. I am reminded of what Thomas Jefferson said when he was asked if he thought he was lucky. "I believe in luck: the harder I work the more luck I have."

Success, much like recovery, is a process. It takes time, faith, and action. Faith is really nothing more than a level of expectancy. If I hadn't had faith I could get sober, I never would have. If I didn't trust my higher power to help guide me through my projects, I wouldn't have the intestinal fortitude needed to persevere when things get tough. I use the spiritual tools I learned in sobriety to keep me calm when things get crazy. I know at a gut level God is guiding my steps. This is very powerful and liberating.

In hindsight, I was very lucky to have become an alcoholic because lessons learned in recovery have given me the tools to succeed in all areas of my life. Luck is nothing more than when preparedness meets opportunity. It's true: some people are luckier than others. The rest of us just have to work harder.

Hire the Best People

An extremely successful entrepreneur gave me this bit of advice. He told me, "People do what you *inspect*, not what you *expect*."

That means even if you hire the best, you still must follow up consistently. This advice works whether you are the CEO of a large corporation or you are simply hiring a teenager to mow your lawn.

The only way to succeed on your project is to train, delegate, and follow up on all the tasks you delegated. You can't do it all. If you are a control freak or an egomaniac who believes no one can do a task as well as you, disappointment is certainly in your future. Unless you are a one-man band, you're going to need help with your project.

In a business situation, make sure that loyalty and a positive attitude are at the top of your list when hiring people to help you reach your destiny. One negative person can contaminate an entire project. It is okay to point out shortcomings and offer alternative routes to success. That is why you hire the best.

It is not productive if someone lives in the problem, or is negative or sarcastic. Negativity grows like a cancer and must be immediately removed. Whenever I hire a new team member, I make sure to schedule him or her to work with the most enthusiastic, can-do people I have on my staff. This ensures that the new staff member gets acclimated to the job and knows what type of attitude is expected while working on my projects. No matter how talented or hardworking people are, if they cannot control their negativity, they cannot work on my projects.

Attitude Starts with You

If you are a leader or would just like to become one, your attitude, more than your words, shows the world who you are. People are always taking their cues from you.

Have you ever noticed that people frequently start looking, speaking, or dressing like their boss? I remember watching the capture of Saddam Hussein's military leaders on TV. It was amazing. They all had the same haircut, mustache, and uniform as Saddam. If imitation is the most sincere form of flattery, Saddam must have been really flattered.

You see this phenomenon played out in every society, at every level. That is why if you wish to lead, if you wish a successful outcome to your chosen project, you must remember that the people with whom you surround yourself will act just like you. If you are sarcastic, they will be too. If you gossip about other employees, they will do the same. If you take your customers for granted, so will they.

Conversely, if you treat every customer as you would your own mother, if you insist on excellence from yourself and all with whom you associate, they will too.

This is where consistency becomes vitally important. People are always sizing you up, just looking for a crack in your armor. To be an effective leader you must walk your talk. Not entertaining petty prejudices and showing respect for all (which includes not dating your subordinates and curbing the use of foul language) must be a standard that begins with you. Whatever you do has an impact and determines what your associates will deem acceptable. So the question is, what type of image do you want associated with you or your business?

What's even worse than having a reputation for being unprofessional is having a reputation for being hypocritical. I remember working for a corporation that would fire managers for dating hourly employees, yet two vice presidents married young salesgirls from the company. The CEO even went so far as to divorce his wife of many years to marry a salesgirl who was younger than his three children.

I am not passing judgment regarding the moral implications of this conduct. I am pointing out that hypocritical conduct is poison to a workforce. It breeds resentment and negativity. People start focusing on these perceived injustices and stop focusing on the reasons they were employed in the first place, which of course was to help customers and earn a profit for the company. (By the way, that company is in dire straits. It was a long slippery slope that took about five years to complete, but that type of behavior and poor judgment spilled over into other areas of the business.)

Keep your standards high. Keep the focus on your project and your business. Keep your personal life out of the workplace.

This list of attributes that I've given you has grown out of years of trial and error. It is a direct result of my exposure to leaders of industry, intense personal struggle, and endless hours of study about how to design a successful life. Reading this book is akin to receiving the answer key to the test known as life. Full recovery is attainable, but not if you wish to cut corners. "Burn your boat" and make a commitment to your project. Assimilating the characteristics outlined in this chapter will shorten your journey to abundance while making the trip more enjoyable. Keep pressing forward.

Let's Review

After working through your goals, you came up with a plan of action and a project that inspired you. No matter what project, career path, or business endeavor you have chosen, a successful outcome depends on your ability to understand and use the following list of principles:

- Think big; never settle for less than you can be.
- Always be a person of excellence.
- Never fear the word *no*.
- Develop discipline; set time aside daily to work on your project.
- Success happens one day at a time; keep a pleasing attitude.
- Be a problem solver. Problems happen, you already know this to be true. Stay calm, ask the right questions, take action.
- Think like a customer. Anyone to whom you give service is your customer.
- Treat customers, employees, and coworkers like partners, because they are.
- Be creative.
- Always keep increasing your knowledge; never stop learning.
- Live and work with enthusiasm.
- Embody character, ethics, and morals.
- Expect to succeed and you will.
- Hire only the best people and treat them like they are the best.
- Attitude starts and ends with you.

FULL RECOVERY ACTION PLAN EXERCISES

Take out your Full Recovery Action Plan. At this point, I would like you to take a moment and put your project down in writing.

What, specifically, is your project?

Why did you choose it?

What do you want to achieve?

Whose help can you enlist in starting your project?

Write out a one- or two-line statement summing up the four previous questions about your project and place it where you will read it daily.

Deliberate Action

Concentration is to bind consciousness to a single spot.
—PATANJALI

NOW THAT YOU HAVE well-defined goals and an inspirational project, it's time for some deliberate action. As I mentioned earlier, some of your biggest character defects can become assets when used constructively and without selfish motives.

Have you ever run out of cigarettes in a place where you could not find one? Have you ever needed a drink or drug and none was available? You can substitute any addiction you may have faced to illustrate this example. If you are or have ever been addicted to anything, you know the intense, single-minded focus you are capable of when necessary.

I have been in these situations and am quite aware of how creative I can be when properly motivated. The difference is that now I use my powers of persuasion and enthusiasm to accomplish my positive, worthwhile goals.

I am not suggesting you be manipulative, underhanded, or pushy in any way. What I am suggesting is that you use the same ability to focus to accomplish your positive, worthwhile goals. If your project and goals are intelligently designed, they will be a benefit to you and all with whom you come into contact.

To live in recovery and enjoy financial abundance, not just spiritual abundance, you must convince people that what you have to give, sell, or offer has value. It must be valuable enough for them to spend their hard-earned money acquiring it.

To live in recovery and enjoy financial abundance, you must convince people that what you have to give, sell, or offer has value.

Take out your Full Recovery Action Plan and keep it handy as you work through this chapter. I'll ask you to complete exercises in it at the end of this chapter, but for now I'd like you to write down the answers to the following questions:

First, you need to get clear on what your product or service is. Who is in need of your product or service? Write down as many potential customers as possible.

If you currently work for someone or are in a corporate setting, at the very least your product is you. Your ability to sell your ideas and value to your employer is just as important as the ability to start a new business or create a new product. We are all salespeople. Whether you're selling the ideas of a good education to your children or selling your commitment to recovery to yourself, how effectively you are able to influence the world you inhabit will make your life either more or less enjoyable.

Do you have any partners, family, or team members who need to contribute to these answers? Don't forget the importance of brainstorming. When you get several people together to exchange ideas, oftentimes new and creative ideas come out of the process. It's important when choosing your team members that they are trustworthy and loyal to the project. Unfortunately, people are human and sometimes don't live up to your expectations. Make sure you do all you can to protect the sanctity of your project. You don't want a misguided associate using your ideas or turning into a competitor.

While thinking about your project, remember this definition for the acronym TIME: Things I Must Earn. Now is a great time to accept the truth that there is no such thing as a free lunch. Success takes time. If you want to live an abundant life, you must earn it.

The idea is not to be pushy, aggressive, or degrading in your approach. Instead, the idea is to offer a solution to your prospects' challenges. Your success depends largely on your ability to satisfy your customers' needs. Any transaction in which you participate should leave all the participants feeling as if they were treated fairly and happier for the experience.

You'll need to address the following questions too as you prepare to sell yourself:

- What do you do well? Where do your talents lie? If you have difficulty deciding, take a look at what you've written in your Full Recovery Action Plan.
- What unique or individual skills do you possess?
- What manners of communication do you employ to encourage people to like you?

- How can you use these God-given abilities to market yourself, your product, or your service?

After you write down the answers to these questions, it's time to look outside yourself.

Ask your family and friends to help you discover your unique and individual talents. Sometimes an outsider, such as a sponsor or mentor, can make you aware of skills you don't even know you possess.

Once you have this knowledge, revisit your project. Ask yourself, how can I use this newfound knowledge to advance my project?

Get Enthusiastic!

Now comes the fun part. It's time to get pumped, excited, and inspired. Excitement is contagious. Start thinking outside the box. Get creative and believe your goal is within reach. Nonconformity is an asset.

Keep focused on your goals and write down ways of attacking your project whenever they pop into your head.

When I was writing this book, I had notes everywhere. I kept a pen and notebook in my truck as well as in every room of my house. Whenever an idea for a subject popped into my head, I wrote it down.

I also had my goals hanging up all over my house. They were taped to my mirror, next to the toaster, in the laundry room, and every other place I frequented daily. Wherever I turned they were staring me in the face. Every day I took time to organize and reorganize my ideas and my notes.

Focus Your Project with an "Elevator Pitch"

An elevator pitch, or an elevator speech, is a concise synopsis of your product, service, or project. It's called an elevator pitch because you should be able to deliver the whole pitch in the time span of an elevator ride, namely, anywhere from thirty to sixty seconds.

This term is typically used to describe the process of an entrepreneur pitching an idea to a potential investor with the goal of selling his or her idea and raising capital. Often, investors will judge the quality of a team and the project solely on the quality of the elevator pitch. Simply said, the people to whom you are pitching your ideas will make snap judgments based on how effectively you can communicate your vision. It allows them to quickly weed out bad ideas and weak teams.

It's been said that some of the most important decisions on the Senate floor have come down to the last whispers of a staff aid to a senator on the short elevator ride down to cast his or her vote.

A variety of other people, including entrepreneurs, project managers, salespeople, evangelists, job seekers, and even speed daters, commonly develop an effective elevator pitch to get their point across as succinctly as possible.

An effective elevator pitch generally answers questions such as:

- Who you are.
- What the product or service is.
- What it does for the buyer or your employer.

Think back for a second to the chapter titled "Fear." In that chapter I suggested not only getting right with your higher power but also working on your physiology and practicing how it feels to be unstoppable. Make sure you add this element to your elevator pitch.

This pitch may be your one shot to get your idea off the ground, so make it compelling, concise, and as enticing as possible.

When I got out of rehab, the job market was extremely tight. At that time, my project was simple: stay sober and find a job with benefits so I could support my family. I had noticed a billboard that was advertising a new store opening a few towns away from where I lived. I can't explain it, but I had a gut-level feeling that I should try to get a job there. I was seeking any advantage, so I typed up a small résumé outlining my previous work experience. The experience wasn't much, but the employment I was seeking wasn't much either. A résumé certainly wasn't expected, but I hoped that because I took the time to be prepared, someone in charge would take notice. I went to the store, filled out an application, handed in my résumé to the service desk employee, and was promptly dismissed.

When I asked to meet with the person doing the hiring, I was told that they were not hiring; they already had hundreds of applications ahead of mine. Don't call us we'll call you. This is definitely not what I wanted to hear. I hate the word *no*. Rather than get defensive, I decided to try and gather information.

Although I was treated harshly, I showed empathy for the overworked service desk employee. I let her know I understood she was just doing her job. I engaged her in conversation, told her of my need for employment, stayed polite, and soon had her laughing. By conversation's end, I had a friend at the service desk. Before I left, she told me she would figure out a way to get my application into the manager's hands.

I waited a day and called the store, but my new friend was not working and no one else would assist me. The next day I contacted my new friend at the service desk who explained that she had someone drop the application on the manager's desk but things did not look good; they were not hiring. I asked for the manager's name, which she was reluctant to give me because he had told her he did not want to be bothered, but after some reassurances, she told me his name.

Now armed with the manager's name, I contacted the office and tried to speak with him, but his secretary kept blowing me off. My goal was to meet the decision maker and convince him that I was someone who could be of value to his organization. I knew I would probably get just one chance to convince him of my value to him, so I prepared an elevator pitch and started rehearsing.

I called the store for two more days before I found someone willing to tell me that the manager was in the building. I drove to the store and all the stars aligned. My new friend was working and pointed the store manager out. As I approached him, he jumped on a cash register and started ringing up customers because although the store had fifteen cash registers and fourteen were open, the lines were still backing up. The place was a madhouse.

I immediately went to the cash register the manager was operating and started to bag for the customers. He was surprised and wanted to know who I was, and I was happy to tell him. I recited my entire elevator pitch without interruption. It was great. I had a captive audience. I told him about my assertiveness, which he was already witnessing. I told him all I knew about the company and their future plans for growth. I was prepared to talk intelligently about the business even though I had never been in retail before. My well-rehearsed elevator pitch and my ability to take action impressed the man. When the lines slowed down, I explained that I had been trying to contact him for days. I told him of my résumé. He invited me back to his office, found my application and résumé already buried under a stack of new ones, and hired me.

My well-rehearsed elevator pitch helped secure me a position that opened the door of opportunity. Once you have summarized your idea into a workable thirty-second pitch, make it your mantra, and practice it every single day. No doctors would think of doing an operation without devoting untold hours to practicing their specialty. They must be sure they are prepared for any potential surprises. No actors would go on the stage without rehearsing their lines. You should not approach your potential customer or end user without thoroughly rehearsing your pitch.

Rehearse in the mirror. Rehearse in the car. Ask friends and family to be your audience and encourage feedback. This is also a great exercise in overcoming fear. If you stumble or miss a line, who cares? You're just practicing. The idea is to make your mistakes when practicing and not on game day.

After you feel comfortable with your presentation, ask a friend or someone in your practice audience to give you a hard time. Tell them to try and stump you. This is another action step in being prepared and conquering fear. When you feel confident and comfortable, it's time for the real world.

Marketing Your Ideas

Gaining an appointment to pitch to your idea can be a frustrating proposition. Like everyone else in our society, employers, corporate buyers, and plain old customers are extremely busy, and quite often have many time constraints.

Always realize, first and foremost, that you are in the people business. People manufacture, sell, purchase, and use any and all of the products and services you have to offer. People want to know one thing: "What's in it for me? How can you help my life be less hectic, more satisfying, and more profitable?"

The ability to reach your full potential is closely related to your ability to meet and communicate with people capable of helping you. You need to speak with the decision maker. I want to show you how the same techniques I used to get my first job out of rehab apply in almost every situation.

The following example applies no matter whom you are trying to meet with. It makes no difference if your project involves solving world hunger, stopping global warming, or selling teddy bears to Toys "R" Us. If your decision maker is in a corporate setting, she probably has a secretary, assistant, or some other type of person that she counts on to run interference for her. Part of this person's job description includes keeping you from meeting with the decision maker. These people are the official guards that you will have to

The ability to reach your full potential is closely related to your ability to meet and communicate with people capable of helping you.

get past to meet the person capable of helping you move your project forward.

I have been on both the buyer and seller side of this situation and understand the frustrations that come with each position. Decision makers are usually under deadlines and time constraints. Assistants are delegated the task of weeding out time wasters. This is why it is vitally important that you have a clear, concise reason for calling and where a well-rehearsed elevator pitch will pay huge returns. You may only have a moment to convince the gatekeeper that you are a person of value who can be of assistance to the decision maker. Your clear, focused professional pitch gives you immediate credibility and can separate you from the other unprepared callers.

Like all of us, secretaries and assistants have good and bad days. If you run into a particularly difficult situation, and cannot get past the guard, it's time to get creative. There are emails, DVDs, product samples, and billboards outside the decision maker's office, and don't forget that most people will sign for a FedEx delivery. There are a thousand ways to contact someone. There is one way in which I can almost assure you that you will never get to meet the decision maker, however, and that is to get on the wrong side of his or her secretary.

Keeping this in mind, you understand the importance of treating these support staff with the respect they deserve. Secretaries are also a wealth of information and they have daily direct contact with the person you are trying to meet. Quite often they can let you know which particular day or hour is the best time to contact your prospect. Many times they are willing to leave information for the decision maker to preview. Support staff employees are a priceless asset.

Whenever you meet a new prospect who can help you with your business, remember to be enthusiastic and sincere. If you are entering your prospect's office, home, or workplace, glance around for possible shared interests. You might notice photos of a spouse or children. Maybe you'll see something such as golf clubs or a tennis racket. These items give you clues to some of the interests of your buyer and will allow you to engage in small talk. This is not being insincere. It is part of the process of getting to know one another. Every friendship you enjoy has come out of shared mutual interests. Don't forget: people like to do business with people they like.

Listening will be key in these meetings. You have five holes in your head; four can be used for gathering information and only one for giving it. As a person interested in selling your ideas, you should keep this in mind. The idea is to gather information and not just simply give it. There is nothing worse than a salesperson delivering a canned presentation.

As you engage in conversation, your goal is to find out what type of space the buyer or decision maker is in today. How is business? What problems are they facing that you can help them solve? Are they under any restrictions that limit the ability to purchase or make a decision today? This process of gathering information allows you to adjust your presentation to your prospective buyer's needs. Never confuse the means with the ends. The purpose for meeting with your prospect is to advance your project or earn money, depending on your project. How you accomplish this is by filling your customer's need for quality goods or services.

Before, during, and after your presentation, keep asking questions. The idea is to create dialogue. You don't want to do all the talking and deliver a monologue. You want the buyer to ask questions. This is why it is so important to rehearse your pitch. If you know your product, answering questions should be easy.

If you are asked a question and don't know the answer, say so. Let your prospect know you will get back to them with an answer. This can work in your favor, because it gives you a reason to follow up with the customer. As you move toward the close, keep asking questions such as these: What do you think of my proposal? Have I given you enough information to make a decision? Then shut up and listen.

If your prospect asks a question, I like to repeat the question back before answering, ensuring that we're both on the same page. By taking this step, I'm sure to meet prospects' needs by giving them an opportunity to correct my perception before I give an answer. I then tailor my answer to fit their needs.

In a corporate setting, the sale or deal is rarely closed at the initial meeting. A good strategy for ending an initial discussion is to find out the names of other people in your prospect's organization he or she would recommend you contact. Often your product, service, or idea affects different departments. It can be helpful to find out what other people in the organization your prospect consults with when making decisions. When you have this information, you can contact each one of them and find out what issues they are facing, and how you can be of service. Armed with a name and a referral from your decision maker, it's usually easier to get a meeting with this "supporting cast" of people.

Once you have had several conversations with the supporting cast, you will possess a great deal of insight that you can utilize in your next meeting with the decision maker. Not only will you feel much more comfortable, because you now have contacts throughout the organization, but you will often have insight that the decision maker himself may have missed. In addition, the decision maker will be much more likely to set up a second meeting, knowing you have done your homework.

Sales is simply finding a need, satisfying the need, overcoming objections, closing the sale, and being rewarded with money for your efforts. No matter what your project is, you will have to sell your ideas to someone. When you ask for the sale, you'll get one of three answers: "Yes," "No," or, "Let me think about it."

"Maybe" or "Let me think about it" is the most common answer. Don't become aggressive or pushy when you hear this answer; rather, keep asking questions. Is there any more information you can provide that will facilitate a decision? Ask when a good time would be to follow up. This is the perfect time to suggest that you would like to find out more about the challenges the prospect is facing by speaking with the associates that are directly impacted.

By asking questions, you might be able figure out what constraints are on the buyer. Sometimes it's as simple as the need to get approval from a supervisor, coworker, or spouse. The idea is to keep the connection open. Even if your customers are not ready to purchase today, they might be ready in six days, six months, or six years from now. Ask when you can contact them again, and follow through.

Next, let's address the "No" response. The inability to handle a negative response is the reason most people fear sales or asking for a raise. From the time you are a small child, you are conditioned to stop when you hear the word *no*. This is a learned response that must be overcome if you want to be successful in any field.

It has been said that defiance is the one characteristic that all alcoholics and addicts share. Now is the time to draw out that characteristic and put it to good use.

While writing this section, I flashed back to when I was in a twenty-eight-day rehab. One of the counselors made the statement, "Out of the fifty people sitting in this room, statistics project that three will stay sober six months, and only one for five years or more."

That got my defiance up. I hate to be told I can't do something. I remember turning to the man sitting next to me and remarking, "Well, it looks like you're out of luck because I'm the one."

After my release, I met an old friend who proceeded to tell me, "You'll be drinking within a week." Statements like these bring out the defiance in me. I stayed sober out of spite. Attending meetings, I would look around the room and tell myself, if these people can *not* drink and drug one day at a time, so can I.

These are examples of turning my character defects into assets. Whenever I hear the word *no* from a prospective client, I think of the word *yes*. I use all that God has given me to achieve a positive outcome. I don't let the word *no* stop me from reaching my destiny. Instead, I use it to leap forward.

I do not torture my prospect or become pushy in any way. I simply learn from the experience, keep the lines of communication open, and move on to the next challenge.

No one can make you feel unsuccessful without your own participation. Even if the answer is no, make sure you keep the connection open. Thank the prospect for scheduling time to meet with you. Then make another call.

If the answer is yes, thank the customer. Always remember

that one of your goals is to be paid. If you do not earn income, you will not be in business for very long. This is why it's important to follow through to the end. Keep in mind that when the customer says yes, it's time to stop selling. Many people talk themselves out of a sale by falling in love with the sound of their own voice. Show some respect for your customers and don't waste their valuable time.

When you leave the meeting, thank God for your success and keep an attitude of gratitude. Remember to follow through on your commitments and treat your customers like the asset they are. Enjoy your success, keep the momentum moving forward, and take another action.

Preparedness and a plan of action are necessary in order for you to become an expert in your field of endeavor. There is no substitute for practice. True professionals practice the essentials on a daily basis. That's how they can perform so well under pressure.

You've no doubt seen a basketball player make a clutch foul shot or a place kicker wander onto the field with seconds left on the clock and kick the winning field goal. These accomplishments don't happen by accident. Being able to perform under pressure is the result of endless hours of practice doing the basics. They make it look easy because they are well prepared. For you to become proficient at the skills presented in this chapter will take the same commitment and perseverance. Deliberate, focused, well-planned action will turn your dreams into reality.

Let's Review

- Define your inspirational project. Be creative and focused, not manipulative.
- Define your customer (don't forget: we all have customers, including employers, students, stockholders, taxpayers, or anyone else you serve).
- Solicit suggestions from all appropriate team members.
- Success depends on your ability to offer service and solutions to your customers.
- Develop an enthusiastic elevator pitch and practice, practice, practice.
- Respect secretaries, spouses, and support staff; they are priceless assets.
- Be sincere. Develop relationships. People choose to do business with people they like.
- Ask better questions and learn to listen.
- Find the need, satisfy the need, overcome objections, close the sale, and earn money.

FULL RECOVERY ACTION PLAN EXERCISES

Now take your Full Recovery Action Plan and write out an elevator speech. The whole pitch should be about thirty seconds long and no more than a minute.

Practice rehearsing your pitch and commit it to memory.

Ask someone to play your audience. When you feel comfortable speaking to your pretend prospect, ask them to play a difficult, rude, or uninterested prospect. The idea is to be prepared.

You'll feel more confident and won't get rattled when you encounter a person who acts this way because you've anticipated their behavior and know how to respond. Pick up the phone and get an appointment.

A Moment of Clarity

A MOMENT OF CLARITY is all it takes for the divine purpose to be revealed. Twenty-four years ago, I woke up in unfamiliar surroundings with no recollection of how I got there. I wandered outside into the sunlight and for a millisecond experienced a moment of clarity that I acted upon. That was the day I surrendered. I admitted I was powerless over addiction and asked for help. That is the day I became willing to listen. During that split second of space between the endless string of my connected thoughts, the grace of God entered my consciousness. The clarity of that moment has changed my world.

We all have experienced such moments of clarity. They arrive as hunches, a gut feeling, or a good idea that pops into your head. It might be the arrival of someone into your life at just the right time, or that twinkle in someone's eye when love comes to call. It's that sixth sense, deep premonition, or feeling of déjà vu that most of us have felt at some time. It is at this time that the universal consciousness is reaching out to us. During these momentary lapses of our ego-based reality, the grace of God enters.

This book is a direct result of a moment of clarity. I was alone in my home. The news was on the television spewing negativity and tales of impending doom. It was a few weeks before

Christmas, and the financial collapse of the economy was in full swing. For the second time in ten years, I had seen my fortune dwindle. The first time was after 9/11, when the stock market collapsed. Following that situation, I became a real estate investor and diversified my investments.

This second economic meltdown not only hit the stock market but also killed the real estate industry. I had a mountain of debt, my construction projects dried up, and an associate of mine had just died. I turned off the TV and pondered my life.

Having done the work of knowing myself long ago, I understood that my higher power built into me the tools needed to not only survive but also thrive in any situation. Fear is not my master. My beliefs and perceptions would not be molded by fear and hysteria, but rather by my faith in God. I decided to relax and meditate. The idea was to calm my mind so that the grace of God would enter.

While I was in a state of mindful awareness, this question came to me: If, instead of your associate, it were you who had died today, what would you regret? What disappointments would you take into eternity? The answer was immediate: I would regret not writing this book. I would regret not sharing a working truth that has allowed me to handle success and disappointment with the same sense of serenity that only understanding the truth could provide.

I have been given more than I will ever be able to repay. I have been saved from the hell of addiction. I have a beautiful wife and son. I have been allowed to experience material and spiritual abundance.

I also have been allowed to experience loss, and though sometimes challenging, it is also a gift for which I am grateful. All the experiences that make up a life allow me to stay connected with the body of humanity. I am an individual, part of the whole. I can relate to my fellow men and women through the gift of compassion that develops from shared mutual experiences. Part of the shared human condition is experiencing loss.

The pain is in the resistance. It is much easier to meet challenges with a hearty yes than to let my ego struggle against life forces that are beyond my control. My business can be an overwhelming success or it might collapse. A relationship may lead to marriage or it may dissolve. Of course, there are numerous possible outcomes for every situation. By accepting this truth, that life happens as it will, I stop my controlling ego from assuming the position of the locus of power. I take the appropriate actions in my life as it unfolds and I leave the results to a power greater than myself. I embrace the fact that I am in control of but one thing: my own choices. I am the cause for the effect the world has on me.

I am not in control of many outside forces such as we all encounter. Natural disasters happen. Economic tides ebb and flow. Everything comes to an end and death is an unavoidable certainty, but how I let these situations affect me is a choice. The Romans had a saying, *amor fati*, which means the virtue of loving one's own fate. This means accepting that whatever conditions you are currently experiencing are not cosmic forces at work sent to make you miserable. They are the same universal experiences that all humanity encounters. The Roman poet Terence wrote, "Nothing human is alien to me."

To embrace this way of thinking requires a moment of clarity. It means responding to life with an enthusiastic yes. A moment of clarity that lets us know there are powers at work that are beyond our egos. They are working in our best interest and for the greater good of humanity. Understanding this is the beginning of allowing Grace into your awareness. Grace brings inspiration beyond logic. Grace points us to truth.

I have experienced many moments of clarity. They were all brief moments of being part of the universal consciousness. The day when, as a sixteen-year-old, I walked out of a liquor store and saw a beautiful young girl pass by whom I had never seen before, yet would later become my wife. The day when I cried out to my Maker after the motorcycle accident that almost ended my life, and the day years later when I turned my addiction problem over to God. The day when I asked a better question and decided to write this book are days when I answered yes to my higher power and allowed Grace to enter my life. What began as moments of clarity has become clarity of vision. A vision once narrowed by small ideas, addiction, and pettiness has grown into a broad view of the horizon and the unlimited possibilities of life.

You and I are kindred spirits. We are willing participants in the game of life. We refuse to sit on the sidelines. We have the ability to take action and we use it.

I would like to congratulate you for reaching this point in *Full Recovery*. I have read a statistic that more than 95 percent of all the self-help books purchased are never read. By choosing to fearlessly press forward, you have placed yourself in the top 5 percent of all who seek a better life.

I encourage you to revisit the chapters in this book regularly when you are seeking fresh inspiration or when you are updating your goals.

Share your knowledge and wisdom and more will be reflected back to you.

Dare to reach your potential.

Believe in yourself and expect a bright future.

Trust the power of prayer to free you from your self-imposed limitations.

Pray for your demonstration.

Listen for direction.

Take action and live a full recovery.

As your consciousness changes, the world around you will change. The Creator has hardwired into you a gift and purpose of which the world is sorely in need. Believe that God is working through you and your blessings will be limitless.

The thought manifests as the word;
The word manifests as the deed;
The deed develops into habit;
And habit hardens into character.
So watch the thought and its way with care,
And let it spring from love
Born out of concern for all beings.
As the shadow follows the body,
As we think, so we become.
—Buddha